ANDRE ST PIERRE

Brutal Truths About Starting a Business: What You Won't Be Told and Need to Know!

How to Guide - Starting a Small Business and Avoiding Critical Mistakes.

Contents

The Brutal Truths About Starting a Business

Starting a business is like jumping off a cliff and building your plane on the way down. It sounds exhilarating in theory—after all, who doesn't want to be their own boss, create something meaningful, and—let's be honest—make some serious cash? But here's the thing: *you're going to crash. A lot.*

Let's talk about the business plan, first.

You've probably heard it a hundred times: "Write a business plan! Get everything down on paper! If you can't plan it, you can't do it!" Sounds pretty official, right? Well, here's the brutal truth: Your business plan is just a fancy piece of paper that will eventually get covered in coffee stains, scribbles, and maybe a tear or two from frustration. Sure, it's important—but it's not a magical roadmap that'll guarantee success. It's a starting point. That's it.

So, here's a better way to look at it: **the business plan is your first draft.** You won't stick to it exactly, and that's okay. If you're reading this, chances are you've heard of "pivoting" (a fancy word for "this is not working—let's try something else") and guess what? It's coming for you, and it's going to hit hard.

Now, let's talk about expectations.

When you start a business, you expect the "start" to be, well, *started*—which makes sense. You have an idea, you've put together a plan (or at least attempted to), and now it's time to turn that into something real. You expect things to go smoothly, to hit some targets, maybe even see a little profit in the first six months. **Wrong.**

What you need to expect instead is a bumpy, sometimes nauseating, ride where things *will* break. Your website will crash, your sales will plateau, and yes, you might spend three hours arguing with your accountant over a tax form you don't even understand. The good news is this: **all of it is part of the process.**

The expectations you have about smooth sailing and quick success? Toss them. A startup is not a one-and-done sprint to the finish line—it's more like a marathon with random obstacles thrown in. And no one talks about those obstacles enough.

Common Pitfalls to Avoid (And How to Avoid Them)

You've got your idea. You've got your vision. Now it's time to roll up your sleeves and get to work. But here's the thing: **you are going to fail.** Don't panic. Failure is not a matter of "if" in business, it's a matter of "when." What separates the successful from the "I-need-to-go-back-to-my-day-job" crowd is how they deal with that failure.

So, let's talk about some classic startup pitfalls.

Pitfall #1: The "I Can Do Everything" Trap

It's tempting, especially when you're starting out. You're the CEO, the marketer, the janitor, the accountant, the everything. You want to save money and do it all yourself. After all, *you* are the mastermind, right?

Here's the reality: **you can't do it all.** It'll burn you out faster than a free trial subscription you forgot to cancel. Eventually, something will fall through the cracks, and it'll likely be something critical, like payroll, taxes, or a key client who just slipped through your fingers. Your business will thank you if you learn to delegate sooner rather than later.

Pitfall #2: Not Understanding Cash Flow

"Cash flow" isn't a fancy business term for "money coming in." It's the difference between living the dream and living in constant fear of your bank account overdraft fees.

If you've got a great idea, great customers, and a snazzy logo, but no cash flow management system? Your business will be toast. You're not just managing *how much money* is coming in; you're managing when and how you spend it. A delay in one customer payment can wreak havoc on your whole month. And if you're lucky enough to land an investor, remember— they *want* to see a healthy cash flow. Not just in theory, but in practice.

Pitfall #3: Ignoring Customer Feedback

Let's say you've spent months crafting the perfect product or service. You've been pouring your heart into this, maybe even ignoring the nagging voice in your head that says, *"What if it doesn't work?"* You launch it, and guess what? No one cares.

The hardest pill to swallow in business is that **your customers are smarter than you.** They will tell you exactly what they want, if you're willing to listen. Not all feedback is useful, of course, but ignoring it entirely is a fast track to failure. If customers aren't buying what you're selling, it's not *them*—it's probably you.

Cold, Hard Truths and Reality Check

Now, for the big reveal: **Business ownership is not all fun and games.** For every inspiring Instagram post about someone who built a six-figure business from their bedroom, there are 1,000 others who are struggling with late nights, unpaid bills, and wondering if they should just go back to their old job. But here's the thing: **It's all worth it.**

Here are the cold, hard truths you won't hear in any motivational TED Talk:

1. **You're going to lose money**—and it will probably be a lot more than you expected. Starting a business is expensive, and it will feel like money is leaking out of your pockets constantly.
2. **You'll feel alone**—the first few months (or years) can be isolating. Even if you have a partner or employees, the weight of the decisions will fall on you.

3. **The stress will affect your health**—it's not all glamour and big meetings. You'll spend sleepless nights worrying about cash flow, clients, and deadlines.
4. **You'll want to quit**—many times, in fact. But the most successful entrepreneurs don't give up; they get creative, they adapt, and they keep going, even when it feels impossible.

But don't worry, you're not in this alone. All businesses go through this, and the ones that make it are the ones who keep moving forward. The key is **staying in the game long enough to get through the tough parts.**

If you take anything away from this book, let it be this: **Business is messy, hard, and full of brutal truths.** But it's also one of the most rewarding things you'll ever do. You'll learn things about yourself you didn't know existed, you'll grow in ways you didn't expect, and—if you play your cards right—your business can thrive.

So, buckle up. It's going to be a wild ride, and you're about to experience the business world like never before. But hey, that's why you're here, right? You're not afraid of a little tough love. Welcome to the world of entrepreneurship.

Now, let's get to work.

Chapter 1: The Reality Check – From Dreamer to Doer

I n this first Chapter we will kick things off looking at gaps between ideas and reality, business research, the differences between being an employee and the boss. As we progress through the Chapter we will start to scratch the surface about some of the truths about starting a business and then really get into the good stuff you need to know!

Understanding the Gap Between Idea and Execution

So, you have an idea. It's a great one—so good, in fact, that it could revolutionize your industry, change the world, and make you rich. You've imagined the headlines, the success, the fame. But here's the cold truth: **ideas alone aren't enough to build a successful business.**

Let's take a step back and look at the journey of turning that shiny new idea into a functioning, profitable business. Spoiler alert: it's not as simple as "just launching" and hoping it works. There's a massive, often-overlooked gap between that eureka moment and actually executing the idea successfully.

Why Ideas Alone Aren't Enough to Build a Successful Business

Here's the thing about ideas: they're a dime a dozen. Everyone has them. But turning an idea into a business? That's a whole different ball game. The idea might be brilliant, but without the right planning, resources, and execution, it will stay an idea. A *nice* idea that never sees the light of day.

The harsh reality: **Execution trumps ideas**—every single time. Every successful business has one thing in common: they didn't just stop at the idea. They took that idea and put in the hard work to bring it to life. They built systems, processes, and structures around it. They made mistakes, they learned, and they iterated. They didn't just hope their idea would magically come together.

Let's look at this with a simple example. Imagine you have an idea for a revolutionary app that helps people manage their personal finances with AI-powered insights. You've come up with the perfect name, logo, and even have a list of potential users who would love it. The excitement is palpable. But here's the problem: **without a clear plan for development, marketing, customer acquisition, and scaling, your app is just a really cool idea on your laptop.**

The lesson? Ideas are just the starting point. The work you put into developing and executing that idea is what will determine whether it flies or crashes.

The Difference Between Innovation and Market Viability

Now, let's talk about **innovation** vs. **market viability**—a common pitfall for many new entrepreneurs. Just because you've come up with an innovative product doesn't mean there's a market for it. **Market viability** is about answering one simple question: *Will people actually pay for this?*

Innovation is about creating something new or improving an existing product. It's exciting, flashy, and, if you're lucky, disruptive. But innovation without market viability is like building a beautiful yacht... on a desert. It's stunning, but there's nowhere to sail it.

Think about the famous example of **Google Glass**. The concept was groundbreaking: augmented reality glasses that could integrate seamlessly with your daily life. An innovative product, no doubt. But the problem? **It wasn't viable in the market.** People weren't ready for it, and it didn't solve a clear enough problem to justify the high price tag. Despite the innovation, it failed to gain widespread adoption.

On the flip side, there are countless examples of relatively simple, non-groundbreaking ideas that succeed because they meet a clear, established market need. Take **Netflix**, for example. It wasn't the first to offer movies or television shows. It was the first to create a viable business model based on streaming content at a reasonable price, backed by a smooth user experience. Netflix wasn't innovative in the *content* sense— it was innovative in the *delivery system* sense, and it hit the market at just the right time.

The takeaway? Innovation is exciting, but **market viability is where the real money is**. Don't fall in love with your idea just because it's cool. Ask yourself: **Who needs this? How does this solve a real problem? Will people pay for it?**

The Importance of Research Before Taking Action

Before you dive in headfirst with your big idea, you need to do something **critical**: *research*. Not just a quick Google search to see if anyone else has tried something similar, but deep, intentional research that answers the hard questions.

Why? Because the worst thing you can do is spend time, money, and energy on a business idea that's flawed from the start. Research doesn't just mean knowing your competition or your industry. It means **understanding the market**, identifying gaps, and confirming that your idea fits a real demand.

1. Know Your Market

You need to understand your target market inside and out. Who are they? What are their pain points? Where do they spend their time and money? What do they *really* want—beyond the surface-level "I want something new and exciting" answer?

- **Market research:** Conduct surveys, interview potential customers, and analyze current trends.
- **Customer personas:** Develop detailed customer profiles to understand their habits, desires, and needs.
- **Customer feedback:** Don't guess. Listen to what people are saying about the problem your idea aims to solve.

9

2. Analyze the Competition

It's tempting to think your idea is so unique that no one else could possibly be doing it. But chances are, someone has already tried—or is currently trying—to solve the same problem.

- **Competitive analysis:** Identify who your competitors are, what they offer, and where they fall short.
- **Strengths and weaknesses:** Understand what your competitors do well and where there's room for improvement.
- **Differentiation:** Know what makes your product or service different, better, or more appealing.

3. Validate Your Idea

Before investing significant resources into your business, validate that your idea is worth pursuing. Can you test it with a small audience before scaling? Are people willing to pay for it?

- **Minimum viable product (MVP):** Launch with a stripped-down version of your product to test demand and gather feedback.
- **Test campaigns:** Run small marketing campaigns to gauge interest.
- **Pre-sales or crowdfunding:** Use platforms like Kickstarter to see if people will pay for your idea upfront.

Closing the Gap Between Idea and Execution

There's a big difference between having a bright idea and turning that idea into a successful business. To bridge that gap, you need more than just innovation—you need market viability, deep research, and a clear plan for execution.

And remember: *research* isn't just about learning the facts—it's about testing, validating, and adapting. You can't just assume your idea will work because it's clever or innovative. You have to dig deeper, understand your market, and refine your idea until it's ready to meet real-world demand.

By the end of this book, you'll know how to avoid common pitfalls, navigate the obstacles, and face the cold, hard truths about what it takes to make a business idea a reality. But first, you have to know that the journey from idea to execution is messy, filled with uncertainties, and requires more than just good intentions. It requires **action**, **adaptation**, and, most importantly, **hard work**. So, let's dive in and start building your business—one small, well-researched step at a time.

The Mental Shift from Employee to Entrepreneur

Making the leap from being an employee to becoming an entrepreneur is like switching from driving a car with cruise control to riding a rollercoaster in the dark. It's thrilling, unpredictable, and a bit nauseating at times. The switch isn't just about changing your title or how many hours you clock in—it's a complete mental shift that will affect every aspect of your life. So, if you think you can keep your 9-to-5 mindset while running your own business, think again. It's time to leave the employee mentality behind and embrace the entrepreneurial mindset.

Adapting to the Mindset of a Business Owner

As an employee, you had a pretty straightforward role: show up, do the work, and collect a paycheck at the end of the month. You probably had a specific set of responsibilities, clear boundaries, and someone else to blame when things went wrong. But as an entrepreneur? You're now the person who has to make everything work.

Welcome to your new reality: You're no longer just responsible for your own tasks—you're responsible for the whole company. This means you have to think in terms of **big picture** strategy, **long-term vision**, and, yes, **constant problem-solving**. The mindset shift is subtle but profound: no one is going to hold your hand, no one's going to give you a to-do list, and no one's going to give you a paycheck unless you *earn it*.

The first thing you need to realize is that **you are not just an employee anymore—you're the CEO of your own company**. That means you need to start thinking like a leader, even if you're still working from your kitchen table in your pajamas. You have to take ownership of your decisions, and this involves several shifts:

- **Taking Responsibility:** You can't pass the buck anymore. If something goes wrong, it's on you to figure out how to fix it. But equally, if something goes right, you get to celebrate those victories, too.
- **Strategic Thinking:** Instead of focusing only on your

12

daily tasks, you need to think long-term. How will your business evolve? How will you scale? What's your plan for the next 6 months, 1 year, and beyond?

- **Embracing Failure:** As an employee, mistakes might have been inconvenient, but there was usually a safety net. As an entrepreneur, failure is part of the process. Learning to embrace failure—not as an end, but as a lesson—is key to developing the resilience needed for entrepreneurship.

The Emotional Rollercoaster: From Excitement to Doubt

Starting your own business is a highly emotional experience. At one moment, you'll feel on top of the world, brimming with excitement about your idea and the future. The next moment, you'll be doubting everything: *Is this really going to work? What if I fail? What if I don't make enough money? What if I've made a huge mistake?*

This emotional rollercoaster is perfectly normal, but **it can be exhausting**. The key to surviving the ride is learning how to manage your emotions and channel your energy into productive action. Here's how:

1. Embrace the Highs and Lows

Starting a business is exhilarating. The highs are like nothing you've ever felt before: the first sale, the positive customer feedback, the first big deal. But just as high as you go, you'll crash down. It's part of the process. **You will feel overwhelmed.**

You'll question your decisions, and sometimes, you might even want to throw in the towel. But **acknowledge** the highs and lows, and remind yourself that both are temporary.

- **Celebrate the victories** no matter how small, but don't get too comfortable—there's always more work ahead.
- **Accept the lows** as part of the journey. Every successful entrepreneur has faced moments of doubt and frustration. The key is to stay focused on the bigger picture.
- **Find support**—whether it's through mentors, fellow entrepreneurs, or friends and family. Isolation can magnify your doubts. Build a support network that can help ground you when the emotional ride gets tough.

2. Managing the Stress of Uncertainty

One of the biggest emotional challenges of entrepreneurship is the constant uncertainty. Unlike your old job, where you had a stable paycheck and clear responsibilities, running a business is like constantly walking on a tightrope. You have to manage cash flow, sales, client expectations, and your team (if you have one) all while juggling the everyday worries of running a business.

The constant pressure to **perform, sell, and grow** can feel overwhelming. That's why learning to manage stress is crucial. Here are some strategies that can help:

- **Establish routines:** Even though your schedule may vary, establishing daily or weekly routines can bring structure to the chaos.
- **Prioritize self-care:** It's easy to neglect your health and mental well-being when you're juggling a hundred things,

but if you burn out, your business will suffer. Make time for physical activity, mental breaks, and rest.
- **Set realistic expectations:** Understand that things won't always go according to plan, and that's okay. There will be months where you make huge strides, and others where you barely stay afloat. Both are normal.

3. Reframing Failure as Feedback

Entrepreneurs experience failure regularly—it's just part of the game. But here's the key: **failure is not the end of the road**; it's an opportunity to learn. Reframing failure as feedback helps you maintain a healthier, more positive mindset as you navigate setbacks.

- **View failure as a lesson:** Instead of focusing on what went wrong, ask yourself what you can learn from it. What could you have done differently? What new strategies can you implement moving forward?
- **Don't take it personally:** The ups and downs of entrepreneurship are not a reflection of your worth as a person. They are simply a reflection of the business environment you're operating in.
- **Keep moving forward:** The most successful entrepreneurs don't let failure stop them. They treat it as a necessary step toward eventual success.

Learning to Be Comfortable with Uncertainty and Risk

As an entrepreneur, uncertainty will become your new best friend. Unlike the comfort of a regular paycheck and a predictable workday, entrepreneurship is full of risks and unknowns. At first, this can be unsettling. But here's the reality: **you can't avoid risk, so you might as well learn to live with it**.

1. Understanding the Nature of Risk

Risk is inherent in starting a business. Whether it's financial risk, reputational risk, or the risk of failure, it's all part of the journey. The trick is not to avoid it, but to understand it and manage it. Here's how:

- **Assess risk, don't avoid it:** Not all risks are equal. Learn to evaluate them in terms of potential rewards and possible losses.
- **Start small:** In the beginning, limit your exposure by starting small. Validate your idea with a minimum viable product (MVP), test your market with pilot programs, and scale cautiously.
- **Mitigate risks:** Understand how to protect your business with proper insurance, legal protections, and a solid financial buffer. Risk management isn't about avoiding risk—it's about minimizing its impact.

2. Building Resilience to Handle the Unknown

The uncertainty of entrepreneurship can be daunting, but over time, you'll develop a resilience to handle it. **Building resilience is about training your mind to accept uncertainty and to make the best possible decisions in the face of it.**

- **Take one step at a time:** When the unknown feels overwhelming, break down your challenges into manageable tasks. Focus on what you can control.
- **Trust the process:** Success doesn't come overnight. Trust that the hard work, even when it doesn't immediately pay off, is adding up to something bigger.
- **Stay flexible:** Be prepared to pivot. The ability to adapt to unexpected circumstances is what will keep you in the game when things get tough.

3. The Entrepreneurial Comfort Zone

Ironically, the more you step into the unknown and deal with risk and uncertainty, the more comfortable you'll become with it. Eventually, the emotional rollercoaster of entrepreneurship will start to feel less like a terrifying drop and more like a thrilling ride. But only if you get comfortable with the discomfort.

- **Embrace the discomfort:** Entrepreneurship is inherently uncomfortable. Learn to tolerate the uncertainty, the risk, and the unknown. That's where the magic happens.
- **Celebrate progress:** Focus on how far you've come, not just on where you want to go. Every small victory is proof

that you're making progress.

- **Push your boundaries:** As you grow, the comfort zone you're in today will be the starting point for the next level. Keep pushing yourself, and you'll keep growing.

Key Message: Mental Toughness is Key

Shifting from employee to entrepreneur isn't easy, and it's not something that happens overnight. But with the right mindset, you can build the mental toughness needed to navigate the inevitable ups and downs. Embrace the uncertainty, learn to manage your emotions, and keep pushing forward—because **you're the CEO now**, and that's exactly what it takes to succeed.

What No One Tells You About Starting a Business

Everyone tells you that starting a business is hard. You hear the cliché: "It's a marathon, not a sprint." They say it's all about the hustle, grinding it out day and night, and eventually reaping the rewards. But here's the cold, hard truth that no one talks about: **starting a business is more than just hard work—it's an emotional and financial rollercoaster that will test every part of your life.** It's not all glory and big paydays. There are sacrifices, hidden costs, and a toll on your personal well-being that you might not be prepared for.

The Financial Strain and Personal Sacrifice Involved

If you're planning on starting a business, you better buckle up. The financial strain is real, and it comes early and often. Sure, we all love the idea of being our own boss, but what's rarely mentioned is that **you might end up working harder than ever—just without the steady paycheck to justify it**. In the early days, your personal savings (if you have any) may be on the line, and even if you've got investors or a loan, the stress of managing your cash flow will feel like an ongoing, relentless beast.

1. Cash Flow is King (And Queen)

Most businesses start off with an unstable cash flow. You might have an influx of clients at first, but there will also be dry spells. The gap between **what you spend and what you earn** can feel like the Grand Canyon.

- **Start-up capital is usually never enough:** Even if you think you've budgeted for everything, unforeseen expenses will arise. Equipment breaks, unexpected fees, and customer delays mean that your initial budget is often more of a guideline than a guarantee.
- **Delayed payments are a killer:** In the early stages, many businesses run on the "promise" of future payments. But delayed invoices, slow-paying clients, and unanticipated expenses mean you could be scraping by for months before seeing a real profit.
- **Personal sacrifices:** With limited funds, you may need to live on a shoestring budget, cutting back on personal lux-

uries (goodbye, Netflix subscription and Sunday brunch) just to keep the business afloat.

2. Giving Up Security for Uncertainty

The financial strain often extends beyond the business itself. When you make the leap from employee to entrepreneur, you're giving up the security of a steady paycheck, health insurance, retirement contributions, and a guaranteed work-life balance.

- **Zero safety net:** As an employee, you had paid vacation days, sick leave, and maybe even a 401(k). As a business owner, those perks vanish. You're on your own when it comes to healthcare, saving for retirement, and maintaining a work-life balance.
- **The emotional cost of uncertainty:** Not knowing where the next paycheck is coming from, how your business will perform in the next quarter, or whether you'll be able to meet payroll—these worries are not just abstract concepts; they are the daily mental load that weighs on you.
- **Family impact:** You may be sacrificing not just your own comfort, but that of your loved ones. The pressure of entrepreneurship can put a strain on your relationship, especially if your family doesn't understand the amount of time and mental energy your new business demands.

The Hidden Costs: Time, Energy, and Social Impact

We all know that starting a business takes time and effort, but here's something they rarely tell you: the **costs of time, energy, and social relationships** will add up in ways you can't anticipate. It's not just about the hours you spend working—it's about what you sacrifice in the process.

1. Time: It's a Resource You Can't Get Back

You may think you're going into business to gain flexibility and freedom. You'll be your own boss! But guess what? **Your time is no longer your own.** You'll be working more hours than you did at your previous job, often for little to no pay at first.

- **The endless to-do list:** There's always something to do—sales calls, customer support, social media updates, product development, inventory management, etc. Your business will demand every minute you can spare, and likely, more.
- **The "always-on" mentality:** Unlike a 9-5 job where you clock in and clock out, your business requires constant attention. You might have to answer emails at 10 p.m., fix a broken website at 2 a.m., or come up with a strategy while on vacation.
- **Time for yourself? Forget it:** The more successful the business becomes, the more your time gets stretched thin. Your personal time, hobbies, and even sleep may be the first things to get sacrificed on the altar of "entrepreneurial hustle."

2. Energy: Your Battery Will Drain Faster Than You Think

Time isn't the only thing that gets sucked away—your energy levels will plummet as well. If you thought you were tired after a long workday as an employee, try running a business where you're responsible for everything.

- **Mental energy depletion:** Entrepreneurs constantly make decisions, solve problems, and deal with obstacles, which can be mentally exhausting. **Decision fatigue** is real. After days of nonstop problem-solving, you'll feel mentally drained and sometimes incapable of making even the simplest choices.
- **Physical energy burnout:** Your body will also bear the brunt of this hustle. You'll likely neglect exercise, eating healthy, and even sleep, all of which are crucial to maintaining energy levels.
- **Creative fatigue:** As the business owner, you're responsible for coming up with ideas, strategies, and solutions, and that takes a creative toll. After a while, you may start to feel like the well is running dry.

3. The Social Cost: Goodbye, Social Life

You've heard it before: "It's lonely at the top." Well, that's because **being an entrepreneur often means sacrificing your social life**. Friends and family may not understand why you can't attend social gatherings or why you're always working. The truth is, while they're out enjoying their weekend, you're working through the night to ensure your business stays afloat.

- **Missed milestones:** While your friends are celebrating promotions or family events, you're often missing those same milestones because you're too busy managing your business.
- **The isolation:** As a business owner, you often spend long hours alone, especially if you're starting from scratch. You might not have a team yet, or you might be the only one running the show. The social isolation can be heavy.
- **Strained relationships:** Your family and friends may start to feel neglected. You might miss birthdays, holidays, or just simple hangouts, and the emotional distance can take its toll on your personal relationships.

The Toll It Takes on Personal Relationships and Mental Health

Starting a business is hard enough, but it becomes even more difficult when it starts to affect your personal relationships and mental health. You're juggling the pressures of the business, the financial strain, and the social sacrifices—all while trying to maintain your mental health and keep your relationships intact. It's a delicate balance, and the toll it takes can be far-reaching. I know from personal experience and have many acquaintances who have had their marriages and personal relationships fall apart while remaining too business focused. Balance is key and strong partners, friends and a support network.

1. Impact on Personal Relationships

The hours you dedicate to your business come at a price—**the time spent away from family, friends, and partners**. As an entrepreneur, it can be easy to become consumed by your work, neglecting those closest to you in the process.

- **Loneliness and isolation:** The intense focus on the business can leave you feeling isolated from friends and loved ones. You may become so consumed by your work that you forget to nurture personal relationships, and they can begin to fray.
- **Relationship strain:** If your spouse, partner, or family doesn't fully understand the demands of starting a business, it can lead to tension and arguments. Balancing business demands with family needs becomes one of the hardest parts of entrepreneurship.
- **Communication breakdowns:** The stress of running a business can make you more irritable, less patient, and emotionally distant, affecting your ability to communicate effectively with those around you.

2. Mental Health Struggles

Entrepreneurship can feel like a rollercoaster—one minute you're riding high, the next you're plummeting into a pit of uncertainty and stress. The constant mental strain, self-doubt, and pressure can take a toll on your mental health.

- **Anxiety and stress:** Constant worry about your business's success, finances, and future can lead to stress and anxiety.

Even small failures can seem catastrophic when you're shouldering the burden alone.

- **Imposter syndrome:** Many entrepreneurs struggle with imposter syndrome, constantly feeling like they're not "good enough" or that they don't deserve their success. This constant self-doubt can undermine your confidence and decision-making.
- **Burnout:** When you're always "on" and never give yourself time to recharge, burnout becomes a real threat. Entrepreneurial burnout is the result of too much work, too little sleep, and no personal time.

Key Message

Starting a business isn't just about the idea, the hustle, or the dream of financial freedom. It's about understanding the **hidden costs**—the financial strain, the time and energy sacrifices, and the toll on personal relationships and mental health. These are the realities that no one tells you about. But here's the thing: **If you can navigate these challenges, you'll come out stronger and more resilient on the other side.** The key is knowing what to expect, preparing for the tough times, and maintaining a strong mental and emotional foundation to keep moving forward.

Chapter 2: Building a Business on Paper – Crafting Your Business Plan

This is a critical Chapter for your startup however it should be understood that while a business plan is a huge foundational piece, it **must be adaptable**. As a business owner there are many variables that are changing continuously including context, environment, threats, clients, political landscape, competitors and technology. Have a solid foundation and be prepared to pivot as needed!

The Importance of a Business Plan

Starting a business without a plan is like setting out on a cross-country road trip without a map or GPS. You might make it eventually, but the journey is going to be far more frustrating, uncertain, and full of detours. A business plan isn't just a formality you fill out to impress investors or secure funding—it's your **roadmap**, your **strategy**, and your **reality check** all rolled into one.

Why Every Business, Regardless of Size, Needs a Solid Plan

You may be thinking, "I'm starting a small business, do I really need a formal business plan?" The short answer is: **Yes.** Whether you're opening a small coffee shop or launching a tech startup, **a well-thought-out plan is the foundation of your business**.

Without a business plan, you risk flying blind. Sure, you might have a great idea or an exciting product, but without structure and strategy, that idea is like a ship without a rudder—it might float, but it won't be going anywhere productive.

1. A Plan Helps You Stay Focused

A solid business plan forces you to think critically about every aspect of your business. It's easy to get caught up in the excitement of launching, but without a plan, you're likely to chase the next shiny idea that pops up. A clear, concise business plan keeps you grounded and focused on the long-term goals, even when you're faced with distractions.

- **Clear direction**: Your plan will map out your objectives and goals, making it clear where you're going and how you'll get there. This sense of direction is vital, especially in the chaotic early days.
- **Prioritize your actions**: The business plan will help you prioritize where to focus your time and resources. It forces you to ask: What's most important right now to move my business forward?
- **Reduce uncertainty**: The planning process allows you

to anticipate potential challenges and risks, helping you prepare better for them, rather than react at the last minute.

2. A Plan Keeps You Accountable

You can have the best idea in the world, but if you don't hold yourself accountable to a plan, it's easy for everything to fall apart. A business plan is your built-in accountability system, guiding you back to your goals when things get tough.

- **Track progress**: Your plan should outline specific, measurable goals. By reviewing your progress against these milestones, you'll be able to see how far you've come (or how far you still have to go).
- **Spot weaknesses early**: A well-constructed plan highlights potential weaknesses and areas for improvement. When you have everything laid out, you can spot problems early and adjust, rather than waiting for them to snowball.
- **Establish a timeline**: Setting deadlines and timelines within your plan creates urgency. It's easy to put things off if you don't have a timeline in place—this is where the business plan helps keep you moving forward.

Key Components of a Business Plan: Vision, Mission, and Execution Strategy

A business plan is not just a collection of numbers and charts—it's the blueprint for your success. It should contain several key components that reflect the essence of your business. These include your vision, mission, and execution strategy. Let's break down these crucial elements:

1. Vision: Where Are You Going?

Your vision is the long-term dream or goal for your business. It's the "why" behind what you're doing—the guiding star that will keep you motivated when times get tough.

- **Think big**: A vision should be aspirational. It's about what you want to accomplish in the next 5, 10, or even 20 years.
- **Inspire others**: Your vision should be something that excites your team, investors, and customers. It's not just about making money; it's about solving a problem or making the world better in some way.
- **Align with your values**: Your vision needs to align with your personal values and the values of your business. If you're passionate about sustainability, for example, your vision should include a commitment to environmentally-friendly practices.

2. Mission: Why Are You Doing It?

Your mission statement is the heart of your business. It explains the **purpose** of your company—the problem you're solving and how you intend to solve it. This is a more immediate, actionable component of your plan.

- **Narrow down your focus**: The mission should be specific and targeted. It's not just about what you offer, but how your product or service makes a meaningful impact.
- **Set measurable goals**: While your vision is broad and aspirational, your mission should be tangible and measurable. What specific problem are you solving? For whom? How will you do it better than anyone else?
- **Engage your team**: A mission that resonates with your team helps create buy-in and ensures everyone is on the same page, working towards the same goal.

3. Execution Strategy: How Will You Do It?

The execution strategy is where the rubber meets the road. It's the practical, actionable part of your business plan—the **"how"** of everything. How will you turn your vision and mission into reality? How will you bring your product to market? How will you generate revenue?

- **Marketing and sales plan**: This should outline how you'll attract customers, build brand awareness, and drive sales. Consider what channels (social media, paid ads, SEO, etc.) and tactics (content, outreach, etc.) will best reach your target audience.

- **Operational plan**: This is the nuts and bolts of how your business will function on a daily basis. It includes everything from staffing needs to supply chain management to customer service.
- **Financial plan**: Your financial strategy should outline revenue projections, funding needs, pricing models, and a break-even analysis. This section is key for understanding the financial health and sustainability of your business.

How a Business Plan Keeps You Focused and Accountable

The best part about having a business plan is that it **forces you to take action**. Without a plan, it's too easy to procrastinate or be paralyzed by fear of the unknown. A well-crafted plan becomes the blueprint for your business's growth, keeping you on track and making you **accountable** to your goals.

- **Clarity and focus**: A business plan helps you focus on what's important. When distractions or challenges arise, it serves as a clear reference point to guide your decisions.
- **Decision-making aid**: When you face tough choices, your business plan can help you assess the situation logically and make the best decision based on the goals you've outlined.
- **Keeping score**: Having specific metrics and goals set in your plan allows you to evaluate your progress over time. If you're falling short, it's a clear signal that you need to adjust your strategy. If you're exceeding expectations, it's a reason to celebrate and think bigger.

Key Message

A business plan is more than just a document to impress investors—it's the **foundation** of your business. From defining your vision and mission to laying out your execution strategy, it's the framework that will guide you through the early stages and beyond. A solid plan will help you stay focused, make better decisions, and hold yourself accountable for turning your dreams into reality. So, before you dive headfirst into the startup world, take the time to **build your blueprint**—your future self will thank you for it.

Market Research: Understanding Your Industry and Audience

Market research is the unsung hero of successful businesses. It's easy to get caught up in the excitement of your big idea—whether that's a revolutionary app or the best new bakery in town—but jumping into the market without understanding your audience and industry is like trying to play poker without knowing the rules. You might get lucky, but more often than not, you'll end up losing your chips.

In this section, we're going to dig into how to **identify your target market**, **analyze your competitors**, **collect valuable data** to validate your idea, and ultimately, understand **your customer's pain points and unmet needs**—because that's where the gold is.

How to Identify Your Target Market and Competitors

Before you spend a dime or lift a finger to launch your business, you need to know **who you're selling to** and **who you're up against**. Think of your target market as the group of people who will benefit most from your product or service, and your competitors as the businesses who are already trying to meet those needs.

1. Defining Your Target Market

Your target market is not everyone. It's not the entire population of the world. Instead, it's a **specific group** of people who are most likely to need and pay for what you offer. Identifying your target market isn't just about demographics like age, income, and location—it's about understanding their **psychographics** too: their lifestyle, values, behaviors, and motivations.

- **Ask the right questions**: Who is most likely to use my product? What are their pain points? What motivates them to make purchasing decisions? The more granular you get with these questions, the better you'll understand your audience.
- **Segment your audience**: Consider dividing your target market into smaller segments. These could be based on things like age, geographic location, profession, or even specific challenges they face. The more you can niche down, the better you can tailor your product and marketing strategy.
- **Create buyer personas**: A buyer persona is a semi-

fictional character representing your ideal customer. It's a way of putting a name, face, and backstory to your market so you can think about them as real people with real needs.

2. Analyzing Your Competitors

Competitor analysis isn't just about knowing who's already out there—it's about figuring out what they're doing well and what they're missing. This allows you to **find gaps** in the market where your business can stand out and offer something better.

- **Identify direct and indirect competitors**: Direct competitors are those offering a product or service similar to yours. Indirect competitors may solve the same problem but in a different way. Both types of competitors are important to understand.
- **Study their strengths and weaknesses**: Take note of what your competitors do well—what are they known for? But also, look for opportunities where you can improve upon their weaknesses. Are their customer service practices lacking? Do they have an outdated website? This is where you can gain a competitive edge.
- **Check their customer reviews**: This is often the most insightful (and honest) data you can find. Read through online reviews to see what customers love and what they hate about your competitors. This will give you direct insight into what your market values and what they feel is missing.

Collecting Data to Validate Your Business Idea

Before you fully commit to your business idea, it's critical to **validate** it with real data. This doesn't mean relying on gut feelings or your best guess—it means collecting insights from your target market and competitors to **confirm** that there's demand for your product or service.

1. Use Surveys and Questionnaires

One of the easiest and most direct ways to gather data from your potential customers is through surveys. Online survey tools like Google Forms, SurveyMonkey, and Typeform make it simple to ask your audience specific questions that will give you real feedback.

- **Ask clear, actionable questions**: Make sure your questions are designed to gather useful data. For example, instead of asking "Would you buy this product?", ask "What problem do you face that my product could solve?" or "How much would you be willing to pay for a product like this?"
- **Test different approaches**: You might find that some customers prefer email surveys, while others engage more with social media polls. Experiment with multiple methods and see what works best for gathering feedback.
- **Incentivize participation**: Offering a small incentive (like a discount or entry into a giveaway) can encourage more people to complete your survey, ensuring you get enough responses to draw meaningful conclusions.

2. Conduct Focus Groups and Interviews

If you want deeper, qualitative insights, focus groups and one-on-one interviews can provide a goldmine of information. These methods allow you to ask follow-up questions and dig into the details of why customers like or dislike your product.

- **Target your ideal customers**: Choose participants who represent your ideal buyer persona. Their feedback will be the most relevant and valuable.
- **Ask open-ended questions**: Encourage participants to elaborate on their responses. For example, instead of asking "Do you think this product is useful?", ask "How would you use this product in your daily life?"
- **Record and analyze feedback**: Pay attention not just to what people say, but how they say it. What excites them? What frustrates them? Look for patterns that can guide your business decisions.

3. Test Your Product or Service in the Real World

Even if you don't have a finished product, **prototyping** or creating a **minimum viable product (MVP)** can be a powerful way to validate your idea. This allows you to collect real data from actual users who interact with your product in the real world.

- **Launch a pilot version**: A pilot version of your product or service allows you to test it on a small scale. This gives you real feedback on the experience, usability, and effectiveness of your product before you scale.

- **Measure user behavior**: If your product is digital, use analytics tools to track how users interact with it. If it's a physical product, observe how customers respond and ask for feedback on specific features.
- **Iterate based on feedback**: Don't wait until your product is perfect. Launch it in its simplest form and use customer feedback to make improvements. This is the lean startup methodology: **build, measure, learn.**

Understanding Customer Pain Points and Unmet Needs

Now that you know who your target market is and have gathered data, it's time to dig into the **real needs** of your audience. This is where you'll uncover **gaps in the market** and find out what customers are truly craving—whether it's a faster, cheaper, or more reliable solution.

1. Identify Pain Points

Customer pain points are the problems or frustrations they encounter that your product or service could solve. If you can pinpoint these pain points, you'll know exactly how to position your offering as the best solution.

- **Look at existing solutions**: Examine how customers are currently solving the problem. What's missing in the current offerings? Is there something inefficient, expensive, or cumbersome about existing solutions?
- **Ask your customers directly**: When talking to potential customers, ask them to describe their biggest challenges in detail. The more you understand their pain points, the

better you can tailor your product to solve them.

- **Read forums and reviews**: Look at customer reviews on platforms like Amazon, Reddit, and niche forums where people are discussing problems that are relevant to your business. This will give you a sense of their frustrations and unmet needs.

2. Analyze Unmet Needs

Unmet needs are the desires or expectations customers have that aren't being fulfilled by existing products or services. These needs often represent opportunities to innovate and differentiate your business.

- **Dig deeper into complaints**: Customers often point out what's missing in a product—whether it's features, quality, or support. Analyze these gaps and see if you can create a better solution.
- **Check industry trends**: Stay updated on trends in your industry. Are there emerging needs or shifts in consumer behavior that haven't been addressed yet? This is an opportunity to meet a growing demand before your competitors do.
- **Focus on value**: When addressing unmet needs, always consider **value**. A customer will be more likely to switch from an existing solution to yours if you offer a better combination of price, features, or experience.

Key Message

Market research isn't just about collecting data—it's about **gaining insights** that will guide your decisions. Understanding your target market, analyzing competitors, validating your idea, and identifying customer pain points are critical steps in launching a business that actually meets the needs of your audience. Remember, a great product or service is only great if there's a market for it. So, take the time to **do your research**—because the data you collect today will be the foundation for your success tomorrow.

Financial Planning: The Lifeblood of Your Business

Let's face it: **money** makes the business world go 'round. Without a solid financial plan, your dream of entrepreneurship is more likely to crash and burn than soar to success. Imagine starting a business with no clear budget or understanding of how much it will cost to run—and then suddenly running out of cash midway through. It's like building a house without blueprints and hoping for the best.

In this section, we'll dive into the fundamentals of **financial planning** for your business, covering everything from creating a budget and forecasting revenue to identifying funding options and managing cash flow. Think of this as your business's financial roadmap—without it, you're just driving blindfolded.

Building a Budget and Forecasting Revenue and Expenses

A budget is your **business's financial GPS**—it tells you where you're going, how long it will take, and what resources you'll need to get there. Forecasting revenue and expenses is about predicting the future, but with the right tools, you can make informed projections that help you stay on track.

1. Creating a Realistic Budget

Before you start spending money on fancy office furniture, marketing campaigns, or that shiny new tech tool, you need a budget that reflects your **realistic** financial situation. It's not just about tracking expenses—it's about planning for what's ahead.

- **Start with fixed costs**: These are expenses that don't change month-to-month, like rent, utilities, and software subscriptions. These are predictable, and they form the foundation of your budget.
- **Include variable costs**: These are costs that fluctuate, like raw materials, commissions, and shipping costs. Be sure to account for these when estimating your monthly expenses.
- **Plan for growth**: As your business grows, so will your costs. Include budget categories for hiring employees, expanding your product line, or increasing marketing spend.

2. Forecasting Revenue

Next up is **forecasting** your revenue—the money your business will bring in. If you don't know how much you're expecting to make, your budget won't be able to balance.

- **Start with realistic sales projections**: Look at similar businesses or industry benchmarks to get an idea of what you might reasonably expect in terms of revenue. Consider how many products or services you'll sell, and at what price point.
- **Consider seasonality**: Some businesses experience peaks and valleys in revenue throughout the year. For example, retail sales tend to rise during the holiday season. Make sure your revenue forecast takes seasonal fluctuations into account.
- **Include contingency plans**: Things rarely go exactly as planned. Having a backup strategy, like additional marketing campaigns or promotional offers, can help boost sales if things go slower than expected.

3. Tracking and Adjusting Your Budget

A budget is not something you create once and forget about. You need to **track** your spending and revenue regularly, adjusting as necessary to ensure you stay on track.

- **Review monthly**: Set aside time at the end of each month to review your actual expenses and income against your budgeted amounts. Are you overspending in certain areas? Are sales coming in as expected?

- **Adjust when needed**: If you notice your revenue forecasts were too optimistic or your expenses were underestimated, make adjustments for the upcoming months. The goal is to keep your business operating at a profit, and that requires flexibility.
- **Use financial software**: Tools like QuickBooks, Xero, and Wave make it easier to track your finances, run reports, and stay on top of your cash flow. Consider using them to streamline your accounting process.

Identifying Funding Options: Self-Funding, Loans, Investors

At some point, nearly every entrepreneur faces the question: **How will I fund my business?** Whether you need money for initial startup costs or to help scale your business, knowing your options—and the pros and cons of each—is crucial.

1. Self-Funding (Bootstrapping)

Self-funding is when you put your own money into your business. It's one of the most common ways to get a business off the ground because it doesn't require giving up equity or taking on debt. However, it can also be risky.

- **Assess your personal finances**: Before you dive into your savings or retirement fund, make sure you understand the risks. Your business may take longer than expected to turn a profit, and you want to ensure you don't jeopardize your personal financial stability.
- **Start small and scale up**: If you're bootstrapping, it's

important to start with a lean operation. Cut unnecessary expenses and keep overhead low to reduce the risk of running out of money.

- **Reinvest profits**: One benefit of self-funding is that you maintain full control over the business. As you start earning revenue, reinvest profits into the business to keep it growing.

2. Loans

Business loans are another option for funding, but they come with responsibilities. Taking out a loan means you'll have to repay the money (with interest), and if things go south, it could affect your credit score and personal finances.

- **Understand loan types**: There are many types of business loans: traditional loans, SBA loans, lines of credit, and microloans. Do your homework to find the one that's right for your situation.
- **Consider interest rates and repayment terms**: Loans come with varying interest rates and repayment schedules. Be sure you understand the full cost of the loan before committing.
- **Have a solid plan for repayment**: Lenders want to know you can repay the loan, so you'll need a solid business plan, including projections for revenue and expenses. The more evidence you can provide that your business is viable, the better your chances of securing a loan.

3. Investors (Equity Financing)

If you don't want to go the loan route, investors can provide funding in exchange for equity in your business. They may bring valuable expertise, connections, and capital, but they also want a share of the profits—and a say in how things are run.

- **Understand equity dilution**: When you take on investors, you're giving up a portion of ownership in your business. Be sure you're comfortable with the amount of control you'll lose.
- **Prepare for due diligence**: Investors will want to dig deep into your financials, business plan, and market potential. Be prepared to answer tough questions and provide documentation of your business's performance.
- **Pitching to investors**: If you go this route, you'll need to perfect your **pitch**. A clear, compelling pitch can make the difference between securing funding and being passed over. Be ready to showcase why your business is a great investment opportunity.

Creating a Financial Safety Net and Managing Cash Flow

Even the best business plans can run into trouble when cash flow is mismanaged. Cash flow is the **lifeblood** of your business, and without a proper safety net, you may find yourself scrambling to cover expenses when things get tight.

1. Establishing a Financial Safety Net

Building a financial cushion for your business is crucial for long-term survival. This is your **emergency fund**—money set aside for unexpected situations that might pop up.

- **Save at least 3-6 months of operating expenses**: Having this amount of cash in reserve ensures you can weather downturns or cover surprise expenses (like an equipment breakdown or a delay in customer payments).
- **Separate personal and business funds**: Mixing personal and business finances is a big mistake. Make sure you have a separate business account and keep your personal savings safe from business risks.
- **Plan for tax season**: Set aside money for taxes throughout the year. If you don't, you could end up with a large, unexpected bill that your business can't handle.

2. Managing Cash Flow

Managing cash flow is one of the biggest challenges for small businesses. If you don't have enough money coming in to cover your expenses, even a profitable business can go under.

- **Monitor cash flow regularly**: Use tools like accounting software or spreadsheets to track how much money is coming in and going out of your business. Knowing your cash flow at any given time allows you to spot potential problems early.
- **Invoice promptly**: If you offer credit to customers, make sure you invoice quickly and follow up on late payments.

Slow-paying clients can cause serious cash flow problems.
- **Control expenses**: Keep your spending in check by avoiding unnecessary costs and finding efficiencies wherever you can. Negotiate with suppliers and look for ways to reduce overhead.

3. Planning for Growth without Overextending

As your business grows, so will your expenses. However, you need to be **strategic** about how you manage growth. Scaling too quickly can put a strain on your cash flow and leave you vulnerable to unexpected costs.

- **Take a gradual approach**: Don't rush into scaling until your business can handle it financially. Expand when you're sure you can support the growth without sacrificing cash flow.
- **Leverage financing for expansion**: If you need to scale up quickly, consider seeking external funding, like a loan or investor capital, to help fund your growth.
- **Use profits wisely**: Reinvest profits into the business to fund expansion, but keep a balance between growth and maintaining a healthy cash flow.

Key Message

Financial planning is not just about spreadsheets and numbers; it's about ensuring your business has the cash flow and resources it needs to survive and thrive. Whether you're building a budget, forecasting revenue, identifying funding options, or creating a safety net, each step is vital to maintaining financial health. Without proper planning, your business could falter—no matter how great the idea. So, take control of your financial future, plan for the unexpected, and make sure your business is built to last.

Chapter 3: Startup Life – What You'll Face Day 1

Overcoming the Fear of the Unknown

S tarting a business is like jumping into an unknown abyss—you can't see the bottom, you don't know if there are rocks or clouds, and you have no idea what you'll encounter along the way. It's no wonder that so many people freeze up, paralyzed by the fear of what could go wrong. But here's the reality: if you spend too much time worrying about the unknown, you'll never take the leap. The trick isn't to avoid fear; it's to learn how to navigate it.

In this section, we'll address one of the most common barriers to entrepreneurship: **fear of the unknown**. Whether it's the fear of making mistakes, the uncertainty of financial outcomes, or simply the overwhelming nature of the journey ahead, we'll explore how to overcome it and take that first, crucial step.

The Paralysis of Perfectionism and How to Avoid It

Let's talk about **perfectionism**—that sneaky beast that keeps many would-be entrepreneurs stuck in an endless cycle of planning, re-planning, and never actually taking action. If you're waiting for everything to be "perfect" before you launch your business, you're going to be waiting forever.

1. Why Perfectionism is a Killer for Entrepreneurs

Perfectionism can lead to **analysis paralysis**—when you overthink everything to the point where you do nothing. Entrepreneurs often get caught in a cycle of tweaking their product, improving their pitch, or optimizing their website, all in the name of making everything flawless. But in reality, waiting for perfection means you're not learning or growing.

- **No product is perfect at first**: Every successful business starts with a rough version of an idea. In fact, many entrepreneurs admit that their first product or service was far from perfect. The key is to get it out there, test it, and improve it as you go.
- **Progress over perfection**: The most important step is not making sure everything is perfect, but getting started. Progress, no matter how small, is still progress.
- **The cost of perfectionism**: Waiting for the perfect plan or the perfect product can lead to missed opportunities, delayed growth, and, ultimately, wasted time and resources.

2. How to Fight the Urge to Wait for Perfection

Overcoming perfectionism starts with reframing how you think about your business. It's about accepting that **imperfection is part of the process**. Start with what you have and improve along the way. Here's how:

- **Embrace the "minimum viable product" (MVP)**: Instead of aiming for perfection, focus on getting something out there that works well enough to meet your target audience's basic needs. You can always improve later.
- **Set deadlines**: Give yourself a timeline to launch, no matter how imperfect your business may seem. Deadlines force you to stop procrastinating and take action.
- **Prioritize feedback**: Rather than endlessly tweaking things, get your product or service into the hands of real users as soon as possible. Their feedback will help you improve much faster than any internal perfectionist obsession.

3. The Secret to Avoiding the Trap of "Someday"

"Someday" is the enemy of entrepreneurship. The longer you wait for the "perfect" moment, the longer your business will stay stuck in your head. It's essential to push past the fear of imperfection and take the plunge—sooner rather than later.

- **Take small, manageable steps**: You don't need to launch the full-scale business all at once. Start small, test your ideas, and iterate from there.
- **Celebrate small wins**: Every step forward, no matter

how small, is a victory. Celebrate the progress, not the perfection.

- **Focus on what you can control**: You can't control everything, and that's okay. Focus on what's within your control and learn to let go of the rest.

Taking the First Step: Why Starting is More Important Than Waiting for the "Perfect" Moment

If you wait for the "perfect" moment, you could be waiting forever. There's never a perfect time to start a business—it's always going to feel like a leap into the unknown. The key is to **take that first step** and start moving, even if the road ahead feels unclear. The longer you delay, the more time you waste—time you could be spending learning, experimenting, and growing.

1. The Power of Momentum

Once you take that first step, everything else becomes easier. Starting is often the hardest part. Once you're in motion, the fear of the unknown starts to fade and you'll gain more confidence. That momentum will keep you moving forward, even when things get tough.

- **Start with a small action**: Don't try to do everything at once. Pick one simple task that will move you forward, even if it's just registering your business name or creating a basic website.
- **Create a routine**: Build consistency. When you make starting a habit, it becomes less overwhelming. Set aside

time every day or week to work on your business.

- **Focus on progress, not perfection**: The faster you move, the more you'll learn. Focus on the next step, not the ideal end goal. Trust that progress will bring you closer to success.

2. The "Fail Fast" Mentality

The best way to combat fear of failure is to **embrace it**. Failure isn't a roadblock; it's a learning opportunity. In fact, the faster you fail, the faster you learn. The fear of failure often holds people back, but in reality, failure is just part of the entrepreneurial journey.

- **Test ideas quickly**: Rather than overanalyzing, test your ideas quickly and cheaply. Get feedback, pivot if necessary, and learn from mistakes.
- **View failure as feedback**: Each failure gives you valuable insights into what works and what doesn't. You can use those insights to tweak your approach and improve your chances of success.
- **Celebrate your failures**: Every failed attempt is one step closer to figuring out what works. Reframe your failures as lessons, not setbacks.

3. Overcoming the Fear of the Unknown

Fear of the unknown is natural—but it's also something you can learn to navigate. The key is to acknowledge it, embrace it, and take action anyway. The unknown will always be there, but if you spend too much time thinking about it, you'll never get started.

- **Visualize success**: Shift your mindset by imagining the positive outcomes of your actions. Visualization helps reduce fear by focusing on what you hope to achieve.
- **Start before you're ready**: There's no perfect moment to start—only the moment you choose. The sooner you begin, the sooner you'll learn and grow.
- **Trust yourself**: You may not know exactly what's ahead, but you have everything you need to get started. Trust in your ability to figure things out as you go.

Developing a Mindset That Embraces Failure as a Learning Opportunity

Failure is inevitable. If you're going to start a business, you'll face setbacks—there's no way around it. But here's the catch: **failure isn't the end**. It's part of the process. In fact, **failure is the feedback you need to succeed.**

1. Reframe Failure as Feedback

Instead of dreading failure, learn to see it for what it is—an opportunity to learn. Every time something doesn't work out as planned, you get valuable feedback that helps you refine your strategy.

- **Failure reveals gaps**: It shows you what doesn't work, so you can adjust and improve. Look at failure as a way to identify areas for improvement.
- **Learn from others' mistakes**: Don't just focus on your

own failures—learn from the failures of others, too. Read case studies, listen to podcasts, and surround yourself with people who've experienced setbacks and come out stronger.

- **Fail forward**: Fail, learn, and keep moving forward. Use the insights from each failure to build a stronger, more resilient business.

2. Cultivate Resilience

Resilience is the ability to bounce back from adversity—and it's essential for success in business. When things go wrong, it's easy to feel defeated, but building resilience allows you to stay focused and keep going, even when the going gets tough.

- **Develop mental toughness**: Strengthen your ability to weather the storms of entrepreneurship. Resilience isn't about avoiding failure; it's about pushing through it.
- **Stay positive**: Positivity isn't just about staying cheerful— it's about maintaining a growth mindset. When you view challenges as opportunities, you're more likely to bounce back quickly.
- **Surround yourself with support**: Build a network of fellow entrepreneurs, mentors, and friends who can offer support and advice when you hit roadblocks.

3. The Power of Persistence

Persistence is one of the most powerful traits of successful entrepreneurs. If you can keep moving forward, even when you're not sure of the outcome, you're on the path to success.

- **Don't quit too soon**: Many businesses fail because their founders give up too early. Keep going, even when things get tough. Persistence is often the difference between success and failure.
- **Setbacks are temporary**: Every setback is just a moment in time. Remind yourself that no obstacle lasts forever and that every challenge can be overcome.
- **Keep your eyes on the goal**: When you feel discouraged, focus on your end goal. Keeping a clear vision of your desired outcome will help you stay motivated, no matter how many failures you encounter along the way.

Key Message

Fear of the unknown is a natural part of the entrepreneurial journey. But if you embrace imperfection, take the first step and develop a mindset that sees failure as a learning opportunity, you'll find that the unknown becomes less scary and a whole lot more manageable. Take action now, and trust that the answers will come as you go.

The Cash Flow Crisis

When you start a business, it's easy to get excited about the idea of turning a profit. After all, that's the end goal, right? But what you *might* not realize is that **profit** and **cash flow** are two very different things—and understanding this difference is critical to your survival as an entrepreneur.

The cash flow crisis is a reality that many entrepreneurs face, often before they even realize it's a problem. Sure, you might be making money on paper, but if your cash isn't flowing in a way that allows you to cover your expenses, pay your team, and keep the lights on, you're in serious trouble. Many startups fail not because they weren't profitable, but because they ran out of cash.

This section will walk you through managing your cash flow, avoiding the most common pitfalls, and ensuring that your business stays afloat when the financial waters get rough.

Managing the Money: Income, Expenses, and Unexpected Costs

The key to avoiding a cash flow crisis is managing your money with both discipline and flexibility. You need to know where your income is coming from, where your money is going, and most importantly, how to handle the **unexpected costs** that will inevitably pop up. And believe me, they will pop up.

1. Understand Your Income Streams

Not all income is created equal. In the early stages of your business, you'll have to focus on making sure you have consistent, reliable revenue coming in. And remember, you can't always rely on a single source of income.

- **Diversify your income**: Don't put all your eggs in one basket. Consider how you can generate multiple income streams for your business—whether it's selling products, services, or even building a subscription model.
- **Know your high- and low-season income**: If your business is seasonal, plan for lean months. When you have good months, stash some cash away for when the market

slows down.
- **Keep track of receivables**: Know who owes you money and when. Late payments can cause cash flow issues, so be proactive about collecting.

2. Keep Track of Expenses

Expenses are the silent killers of a business. While it's easy to get excited about bringing in money, it's even easier to start spending it. You need to track your expenses carefully to ensure you're not running your business into the ground before it's even gotten started.

- **Fixed vs. variable expenses**: Fixed costs (like rent and salaries) are easy to predict, but variable costs (like raw materials or marketing) can fluctuate. Make sure you track both carefully.
- **Cut unnecessary expenses**: In the early stages of your business, it's easy to overspend on things that don't directly contribute to growth. Be ruthless in identifying which expenses are essential.
- **Have a budget for "surprises"**: Things will break, employees will ask for raises, or an emergency will crop up. Create a cushion in your budget for these unexpected costs.

3. Prepare for the Unexpected

Here's the harsh reality: no matter how well you plan, something unexpected will happen. The sooner you come to terms with this, the better prepared you'll be. The best way to handle the unknown is to build contingencies into your cash flow strategy.

- **Emergency fund**: Set aside a percentage of your revenue for emergencies. Having cash on hand for the inevitable surprises (like unexpected repairs, legal fees, or a market downturn) will make all the difference.
- **Flexible spending**: Know where you can cut back if necessary. Flexibility in your spending can keep you from running into cash flow problems.
- **Track your cash flow constantly**: Don't wait for the end of the month to check your finances. Monitoring your cash flow in real-time will help you catch problems before they get out of hand.

Understanding the Difference Between Profit and Cash Flow

It's critical to understand that **profit** and **cash flow** are not the same thing. You could be showing a profit on paper and still run out of cash. Here's how:

1. Profit Is Not the Same as Cash Flow

Profit refers to the difference between your income and expenses at the end of a given period. Cash flow, however, refers to the actual movement of money in and out of your business over time.

- **Profit is about accounting**: Profit takes into account revenue minus expenses, but it doesn't always reflect the reality of your cash position. You might have a profitable month, but if your clients haven't paid, your cash flow could be negative.

- **Cash flow is about liquidity**: Cash flow is what allows you to pay your bills, employees, and other obligations. Even if you're profitable on paper, if cash isn't coming in when you need it, you're in trouble.
- **Don't mistake "paper profit" for cash in hand**: A business can show a profit but still struggle with cash flow if they have a lot of outstanding invoices or high costs that aren't immediately covered.

2. Managing Cash Flow: Cash Is King

Cash flow management is one of the most important aspects of running a successful business. You can be profitable and still find yourself unable to pay bills, which can lead to huge problems down the road.

- **Timing is everything**: Managing cash flow is all about timing. You need to be able to predict when your revenue will come in and when your expenses will go out. If there's a gap between the two, you need to plan accordingly.
- **Focus on net cash flow**: Your business may make a large profit, but if it's not translating into positive cash flow, you have a problem. Always track the cash in vs. cash out for a clear picture of your financial health.
- **Invoice quickly, pay slowly**: Speed up your invoicing process to ensure that your cash flow stays steady. If possible, negotiate payment terms with your suppliers to ensure that you're not paying out faster than money is coming in.

3. Tools to Track Cash Flow

The best way to stay on top of cash flow is to use proper tools and systems. Don't rely on a vague mental picture of your finances—get organized and keep detailed records.

- **Use accounting software**: QuickBooks, Xero, or Fresh-Books are all great tools to keep track of your income and expenses in real-time. They can help you generate accurate financial statements and manage cash flow effectively.
- **Create a cash flow forecast**: Forecast your cash flow for at least 3–6 months in advance. This gives you a heads-up about potential issues and allows you to plan for periods of low cash flow.
- **Hire an accountant or financial advisor**: If managing cash flow isn't your strong suit, consider bringing in a professional. An accountant can help you get a clearer picture of your financial health and avoid expensive mistakes.

How to Prevent Running Out of Money in the Early Stages

Early-stage businesses are especially vulnerable to running out of cash. Without a steady stream of revenue and a clear understanding of cash flow, many startups collapse before they even have a chance to grow. But with some careful planning, you can avoid this pitfall.

1. Build a Buffer into Your Budget

You can't predict every cost, but you can anticipate the need for some leeway. Build a financial cushion into your business plan to account for the unexpected.

- **Set aside 3–6 months of operating expenses**: This will give you the breathing room you need if your revenue dips or if costs rise unexpectedly.
- **Don't overestimate income**: It's easy to get excited and forecast overly optimistic revenue projections. Be conservative and allow for lower-than-expected sales.
- **Plan for lean periods**: Make sure you're budgeting for months when sales might be slower or more inconsistent.

2. Maintain a Lean Operation

Start with a lean approach and only scale when the money is there to support it. This will allow you to keep your expenses low while you fine-tune your business model.

- **Outsource instead of hiring full-time staff**: In the beginning, try outsourcing or using freelancers for specific tasks to avoid committing to a full-time salary.
- **Avoid unnecessary expenses**: Cut back on non-essential costs like fancy office space or lavish marketing campaigns. Keep things simple and direct.
- **Negotiate with suppliers**: Work with suppliers to extend payment terms or negotiate better prices. This can help you keep cash flow steady while your business ramps up.

3. Monitor Your Cash Flow Daily

You don't need to become obsessed with every penny, but you should always know where you stand financially. Regularly monitor your cash flow to make sure you're not heading for trouble.

- **Review financials weekly**: Track your cash inflow and outflow each week to identify any potential issues before they escalate.
- **Use cash flow reports**: Regularly update your cash flow forecast and compare it with your actual income and expenses.
- **Stay alert to changes**: If you notice a dip in cash flow, take action immediately. The sooner you catch a problem, the easier it will be to fix.

Key Message

Managing cash flow is one of the most difficult and essential aspects of building a business. But if you can master it early on, you'll have the financial stability you need to survive the ups and downs of entrepreneurship. With careful planning, timely action, and the right mindset, you can prevent the dreaded cash flow crisis from derailing your business.

Dealing with Burnout: The Entrepreneur's Silent Killer

As an entrepreneur, the pressure to succeed is relentless. Every day feels like a race against the clock, with a never-ending list of things to do. You're juggling marketing, sales, operations, customer service, and, let's not forget, the financials. And that's all before you even start thinking about growth and innovation.

But here's the brutal truth: **working yourself to the bone isn't a badge of honor.** It's a fast track to burnout, and it will catch up with you when you least expect it.

Burnout is the silent killer of businesses—especially in the early stages. You pour your heart and soul into your business, often sacrificing your mental health, personal relationships, and physical well-being in the process. But if you don't recognize the signs of burnout and take action to protect yourself, you'll find that your business will crumble—not because it wasn't a great idea, but because you couldn't keep going long enough to see it through.

In this section, we'll discuss how to **recognize burnout**, **why working non-stop is a terrible strategy**, and most importantly, how to **set boundaries and manage stress** so that you can stay in the game long-term.

Recognizing the Signs of Burnout in Yourself and Your Team

Burnout isn't always obvious, and it often sneaks up on you until it's too late. But there are signs you can look for—both in yourself and your team—that will help you catch burnout before it takes over.

1. Physical and Emotional Exhaustion

When you start to feel like your energy is constantly depleted, and no amount of sleep or coffee can bring you back to life, you're likely in burnout territory.

- **Chronic fatigue**: If you're tired all the time, no matter how much sleep you get, that's a major red flag. When burnout sets in, your body is constantly in a state of stress, and it depletes your energy reserves.
- **Emotional numbness**: You're no longer excited about your business. What once felt like a thrilling venture has turned into an exhausting obligation. You might also feel irritable or disconnected from the work that once fueled you.
- **Physical symptoms**: If your body starts showing physical signs of stress—headaches, back pain, frequent illness, or even trouble sleeping—it's a clear indication that burnout is lurking.

2. Declining Productivity

When you're burnt out, your productivity takes a nosedive. The longer you push through, the harder it becomes to keep up with tasks, and the lower the quality of your work becomes.

- **Procrastination**: What used to be a simple task now feels insurmountable. You delay decisions and avoid tasks altogether because your mental energy is spent on managing stress and fatigue.
- **Mistakes and oversights**: When you're tired and distracted, it's easy to miss details, overlook important issues, or make errors you wouldn't typically make. This can lead to bigger problems down the line.
- **Lack of innovation**: If you're no longer excited about brainstorming new ideas or pushing the business forward, it's a sign you're losing the spark. Creativity and fresh ideas are often the first casualties of burnout.

3. Team Burnout

Burnout doesn't just affect the business owner. If you have a team, it can affect them too. A leader who is burnt out often sets the tone for the whole company.

- **Increased absenteeism**: If your team members are starting to miss work frequently, or if they seem disengaged and less enthusiastic, it could be a sign of burnout.
- **Negative atmosphere**: Burnout tends to breed negativity. If morale is low, if you or your team members are feeling disconnected from the company's mission, or if the work

environment has become toxic, burnout might be the cause.

- **High turnover**: A burned-out team will start to look for ways out. High turnover rates are often a sign that people are not only tired but emotionally drained and disconnected from their work.

Why Working "Around the Clock" Is Unsustainable and Counterproductive

You may be tempted to push yourself (and your team) beyond human limits, thinking that working around the clock is the key to success. But the reality is, working non-stop is not only unsustainable, it's also counterproductive in the long run.

1. Diminishing Returns

The longer you work without breaks, the more inefficient you become. It's like driving a car without stopping for gas—you'll eventually run out of fuel. Working long hours may give you a temporary sense of productivity, but as fatigue sets in, your output quality and decision-making ability decrease.

- **Declining focus**: As fatigue sets in, your focus becomes scattered. You start losing concentration and making poor decisions because you can't maintain your attention on critical tasks.
- **Reduced problem-solving ability**: When you're exhausted, your brain doesn't have the bandwidth to come up with creative solutions to problems. The simple solutions start to feel difficult, and the complex ones become nearly impossible.

- **Lower productivity per hour**: Studies show that productivity actually drops after a certain number of hours worked per week, especially if those hours aren't balanced with proper breaks and downtime.

2. Long-Term Health Consequences

Pushing yourself too hard is bad for your body. The effects of chronic stress, sleep deprivation, and overwork can lead to long-term health problems such as high blood pressure, heart disease, and mental health issues like anxiety and depression.

- **Sleep deprivation**: Entrepreneurs often sacrifice sleep to get ahead, but lack of sleep affects memory, decision-making, and cognitive function. It also weakens your immune system, making you more susceptible to illness.
- **Increased risk of chronic illness**: Chronic stress can trigger physical problems, including cardiovascular issues and digestive problems. Prolonged overwork can increase your risk for long-term health problems.
- **Mental burnout**: Stress and overwork don't just take a toll on your body; they can also lead to mental health issues like anxiety, depression, and burnout that could take years to recover from.

3. Impact on Relationships

Your business is important, but it shouldn't come at the expense of your relationships. Whether it's with family, friends, or your team, burnout can create a rift in personal and professional connections.

- **Strained relationships**: When you're constantly consumed by your business, you may begin to neglect personal relationships. You're too tired or stressed to spend time with loved ones, which can cause resentment.
- **Work-life imbalance**: Entrepreneurs often struggle to find balance, but working around the clock will eventually isolate you from other aspects of life. The need for social interaction, hobbies, and relaxation is just as important for your well-being as the business itself.
- **Leadership erosion**: If you're always tired, burned out, or emotionally drained, your leadership will suffer. Your team will notice if you're disconnected, unenthusiastic, or short-tempered, which can cause them to lose respect or motivation.

Setting Boundaries and Managing Stress as a Business Owner

One of the most important things you can do as an entrepreneur is **set clear boundaries**. This means knowing when to say "no," how to prioritize your health and relationships, and taking the necessary steps to recharge so that you can continue to build your business with energy and enthusiasm.

1. Schedule Downtime and Stick to It

You need breaks, just like your employees. In fact, you need them more, because you're responsible for leading the whole ship.

- **Plan your personal time**: Schedule breaks, family time, vacations, and even "me time" just like you would a business meeting. Treat it as non-negotiable.
- **Take regular vacations**: Get away from the business for a few days or a week. You might think you can't afford it, but you can't afford not to. Time away will help you recharge and come back with fresh ideas.
- **Use weekends to unplug**: Treat weekends as a time to step away from work entirely. Use this time to relax, enjoy your personal life, and reset your energy.

2. Delegate and Outsource

You don't have to do it all yourself. In fact, if you try, you're setting yourself up for failure. Build a team that you can trust, and delegate the work.

- **Hire the right people**: If you can afford it, hire employees or freelancers to take over tasks that drain you or that aren't part of your core skills.
- **Outsource when needed**: Use outsourcing platforms for tasks like bookkeeping, marketing, or customer service. This will allow you to focus on the high-level strategy.
- **Delegate responsibilities**: Don't micromanage your team. Trust them to do their job, and let them handle the day-to-

day so you can focus on what matters most.

3. Develop Stress Management Techniques

Stress is inevitable, but it doesn't have to break you. Developing strategies to manage stress is crucial for long-term success and personal well-being.

- **Exercise regularly**: Physical activity is one of the best ways to relieve stress. Whether it's a walk, a gym session, or yoga, make exercise a regular part of your routine.
- **Practice mindfulness**: Meditation, deep breathing exercises, or even just taking a few minutes to clear your head can help you stay centered when things get hectic.
- **Set realistic goals**: Don't try to do everything at once. Break your business goals into manageable tasks and celebrate small wins. This will help reduce stress and keep you motivated.

Key Message

Burnout isn't just a buzzword—it's a real, dangerous phenomenon that affects countless entrepreneurs. But with a little awareness and some proactive measures, you can keep burnout at bay and create a sustainable business that doesn't sacrifice your health, relationships, or sanity. **Take care of yourself first, your clients will be happy and your business will thrive!**

CHAPTER 3: STARTUP LIFE – WHAT YOU'LL FACE DAY 1

Chapter 4: Navigating Common Pitfalls – Lessons from Entrepreneurs Who Failed

Underestimating the Time Commitment

If you're entering the world of entrepreneurship with the belief that you can build a successful business in a few months, I have some hard news for you: **you're wrong.** Sure, we all hear stories about overnight successes—companies that seem to come out of nowhere, explode in popularity, and make their founders millionaires. But here's the brutal truth: **for every overnight success, there are thousands of businesses grinding away in the trenches, year after year, without the fanfare.**

The reality is, starting and running a business takes *way* longer than most people realize. And if you underestimate the time commitment, you'll set yourself up for frustration, burnout, and, eventually, failure. But it doesn't have to be this way. By understanding the time investment required and adjusting your expectations, you can navigate the long journey of entrepreneurship more successfully.

Let's take a closer look at what it really takes to launch and run a business, why the "overnight success" myth is misleading, and how to manage your time and expectations as you build your empire.

How Long It Really Takes to Launch and Run a Successful Business

When you have a great idea, it's easy to assume that success is just around the corner. After all, how hard can it be to get things off the ground, right? But the truth is that business success isn't instantaneous. Here's a look at the timeline most entrepreneurs can expect:

1. Idea Validation and Market Research (3–6 months)

Before you even start building your product or service, you need to spend time validating your idea. The idea may seem great in theory, but does it hold up in the real world? Can it solve a significant problem for a specific audience?

- **Survey your target market**: Get feedback from real potential customers. Conduct surveys, talk to industry experts, and gather data to ensure there's a genuine need for your product.
- **Competitive analysis**: Identify who your competitors are, how they operate, and what they're doing right (and wrong). This will give you valuable insights into where your business can fit in.
- **Adjust your concept**: Based on your findings, you may need to tweak your idea or pivot entirely. Market research

is a crucial first step, but it can be time-consuming and requires patience.

2. Product Development and Testing (6–12 months)

Once your idea is validated, it's time to start developing your product or service. Whether you're building software, designing a physical product, or creating a service, this is where the real work begins.

- **Prototype, iterate, and test**: Develop an initial version of your product and test it with real users. Expect to go through multiple iterations to improve your offering.
- **Customer feedback**: Early feedback from your customers is essential to ensure you're meeting their needs. Adjust your product or service based on this input.
- **Legal and logistical steps**: Depending on your business type, you may need time for legal setups (trademarks, patents, incorporation) and logistics (supply chain, manufacturing, or service delivery infrastructure).

3. Marketing and Sales Ramp-Up (1–2 years)

Even if you've created a great product, you won't sell anything unless you put effort into marketing and building a customer base. Don't expect to get rich quick. A robust marketing strategy takes time to develop and implement.

- **Building brand awareness**: At first, you'll be focused on building awareness through digital marketing, word of mouth, social media, and paid ads. But this doesn't happen overnight.

- **Customer acquisition**: Attracting and converting leads into customers takes time. Your sales processes will need refining, and even a small conversion rate can make a big difference in the beginning.
- **Scaling slowly**: As you start to see success with your marketing efforts, scaling up your business will take additional time. Expanding into new markets, hiring staff, and increasing production capacity all take time, effort, and investment.

4. Ongoing Operations and Long-Term Growth (Ongoing)

Once you've got the basics down and your business is running, you'll enter the phase of steady operations and long-term growth. But this doesn't mean you can take a break—growth demands constant attention.

- **Monitoring cash flow and profitability**: Managing money and ensuring profitability is an ongoing responsibility. Even established businesses can run into cash flow problems if they're not carefully managed.
- **Customer retention**: In many industries, the real money comes from repeat customers. Building and maintaining customer loyalty takes time and continuous effort.
- **Innovation and adaptation**: As the market evolves, so must your business. This requires ongoing research and development to stay ahead of the curve and keep up with changing customer preferences.

The Myth of the "Overnight Success" and Why It's Misleading

It's easy to fall for the idea that businesses that explode in success are just a flash in the pan—some big idea that hit the right trend at the right moment. The stories of startups that seem to come from nowhere and go viral overnight are exciting, but they are **the exception, not the rule**.

In reality, behind every "overnight success" is **years of grinding**. For every Facebook, Instagram, or Airbnb, there are countless businesses that started slow, encountered tons of obstacles, and struggled to break even in the early years. It's not that these businesses weren't great ideas—it's just that success didn't happen immediately.

1. The Time Behind the Hype

Take the famous case of Instagram. When Instagram launched, it didn't skyrocket to success overnight. The app went through multiple versions before finding its market fit. Founder Kevin Systrom spent over two years working on the app before it was even noticed.

- **Early failures**: The first version of Instagram was not the app it is today. It was a simple photo-sharing app with no social network features, and the founders had to make several pivots to make it work.
- **Slow user growth**: In the early days, Instagram didn't get millions of downloads. It grew slowly, adding more features and improving the user experience over time.

2. The Media Loves a Good Story, Not the Truth

The media loves to tell stories of overnight success because they're exciting. But behind every success story, there's a backstory of frustration, doubt, and months—if not years—of hard work and struggle.

- **The "overnight" illusion**: In reality, businesses that gain traction quickly often do so after years of building and refining their products, networks, and marketing strategies.
- **Timing and luck**: Many businesses owe part of their success to being in the right place at the right time. For example, companies that launched during a period of technological boom or market change often saw explosive growth—but only because they'd been working for years behind the scenes to build a solid foundation.

3. It's Not About a Big Break—It's About Consistency

The truth is, you don't need to "get lucky" or wait for a big break. You just need to be **consistent**.

- **Small wins compound**: Every sale, every new customer, every positive review matters. Success doesn't come from one huge event—it comes from consistent effort over time.
- **Staying the course**: While some businesses might experience a sudden spike, most entrepreneurs build their success steadily. If you remain focused on your goals, continue iterating and improving, and keep learning, your business will grow.

Managing Your Expectations and Finding Balance

One of the most important things you can do when starting a business is to **manage your expectations**. Business growth takes time. You'll have setbacks. You'll make mistakes. Some days, you'll feel like you're not getting anywhere.

But that's normal.

1. Understand the Long-Term Commitment

Know that success won't happen overnight. The early days of your business will require patience, perseverance, and a willingness to adapt. Managing your expectations helps you avoid the frustration of feeling like you're not moving fast enough.

- **Celebrate small milestones**: Instead of expecting instant success, set smaller, achievable goals. Celebrate when you hit milestones—whether it's getting your first sale, hitting your first month of profitability, or gaining your first loyal customer.
- **Focus on progress, not perfection**: The perfect product doesn't exist, and you'll never have everything in place. Focus on progress, not perfection, and remember that you're building something over time, not in a single day.

2. Embrace the Slow Build

A business is like a garden. It doesn't grow overnight, but if you water it, nurture it, and give it time, it will eventually flourish. The slow build is part of the process.

- **Don't rush the process**: Some things can't be rushed. The market takes time to respond, customers take time to trust you, and growth takes time to sustain. Enjoy the process of building.
- **Be patient**: If you want overnight success, you might end up frustrated. But if you focus on steady, long-term growth, you'll find that your business starts to snowball.

3. Avoid Burnout by Setting Realistic Goals

If you push yourself too hard, you'll burn out. If you're always expecting overnight success, you'll be disappointed and overworked. Balance your drive with realistic goals and allow yourself to take breaks when needed.

- **Set achievable daily, weekly, and monthly goals**: Breaking down your long-term goals into smaller, achievable steps will help you stay on track and prevent overwhelm.
- **Give yourself grace**: Understand that not everything will go as planned. Allow yourself to adjust and learn from mistakes without being overly critical.

Key Message

Starting a business takes more time than you think—but that's okay. The process of growth, learning, and adapting is what makes entrepreneurship so rewarding. It makes sense to keep all of your options open such as starting the business part-time while having a secondary source of income. You can jump straight in but be sure to do your research and follow your plan. Whatever you choose, embrace the journey, set realistic expectations, and you'll be amazed at how far you can go!

Ignoring Customer Feedback

As an entrepreneur, it's easy to fall in love with your own idea. After all, you've put time, energy, and heart into it. But here's the thing: **your business isn't about your idea—it's about your customer.** Ignoring their feedback is like trying to drive a car with your eyes closed. You might get somewhere, but you're bound to crash.

The brutal truth is that **continuous feedback and iteration** are essential for the survival and growth of your business. You can't assume you know what your customers want based on your own preferences or assumptions. **Real data**—and real customer insights—are what will shape your product, refine your service, and ensure you're meeting the actual needs of the market.

This section is all about why ignoring customer feedback is a fatal mistake, how to use it to improve your business, and why testing your product or service early on is crucial for long-term success.

The Importance of Continuous Feedback and Iteration

Building a business is an ongoing process of learning, adapting, and evolving. **Customer feedback is the compass that helps you steer the ship**—if you ignore it, you're sailing blind. Let's break down the importance of feedback and how it helps refine your business:

1. Your Customers Know Best

Customers are the lifeblood of your business. They interact with your product or service daily, and they see things you might not. By seeking out their opinions, you're gaining insights into what works, what doesn't, and where improvements can be made.

- **Customer feedback channels**: Whether through surveys, online reviews, or social media comments, make it easy for your customers to provide feedback. The more channels you have, the more data you can gather.
- **Listening to complaints**: Complaints often highlight areas for improvement. If customers are consistently pointing out a flaw, don't brush it off—address it head-on. A small fix could drastically improve your product and customer satisfaction.

2. Validating Assumptions

As an entrepreneur, you're bound to have assumptions about what your customers want or how your business should be structured. However, assumptions are dangerous. They can lead you down the wrong path, wasting time and resources. Feedback validates your assumptions—and helps you adjust course when necessary.

- **Survey your target market**: Don't wait for customers to come to you with feedback. Actively seek it out.

Before launching a new feature or product, ask your target audience if it's something they want.

- **Analyze customer behavior**: Look beyond what people say to what they actually do. Analyze how customers are interacting with your website, app, or service. If they're not taking the actions you expect, there's a reason for that.

3. Iteration: The Key to Constant Improvement

Customer feedback isn't a one-and-done exercise. It's an ongoing process. Feedback allows you to **iterate**—make small changes and improvements over time. These tweaks can have a huge impact on the customer experience and your business's success.

- **A/B testing**: Run experiments with different versions of your product or marketing materials. Use customer data to determine which version works better.
- **Continuous product updates**: Don't assume your product is "done" once it's launched. Continuous improvement is key to maintaining a competitive edge.

How to Test Your Product or Service Before Going All-In

You don't have to bet everything on your first attempt. In fact, **you shouldn't.** Testing your product or service before going all-in is one of the smartest things you can do as an entrepreneur. By piloting your idea, you can uncover potential flaws, refine your offering, and validate your business concept without committing all your time, money, and energy upfront.

1. Start Small: The Power of a Minimum Viable Product (MVP)

Instead of spending months or even years developing a fully-fledged product, create a **minimum viable product (MVP)**—a simplified version that allows you to test your core idea without the bells and whistles. An MVP is designed to validate the key assumptions about your business idea with the least amount of effort and cost.

- **Get real-world feedback**: Your MVP is an opportunity to gather feedback from early adopters—people who are willing to test your product in its rawest form. Use this feedback to improve your product before committing further resources.
- **Focus on core features**: Don't try to make your MVP perfect. Focus on the key features that solve your customers' pain points. Once you validate those, you can expand and enhance your product.

2. Pilot Programs and Beta Testing

Running a **pilot program** or offering **beta testing** to a select group of customers is another great way to test your product before launch. This controlled environment lets you get detailed feedback from a group of users without putting your product in front of the masses.

- **Engage your target market**: Select beta testers who match your ideal customer profile. These are the people who will give you the most valuable insights into your product's strengths and weaknesses.

- **Ask the right questions**: Use structured surveys and open-ended questions to gather feedback on usability, functionality, and overall experience. This will help you make targeted improvements.

3. Adjust Based on Data, Not Gut Feelings

Don't rely on your intuition or personal biases when making decisions about your product. Trust the data that comes from testing. If customers don't like a feature or find it confusing, don't assume they're wrong—**they're telling you something valuable.**

- **Look for patterns**: Collect data from a variety of sources (surveys, customer reviews, analytics) and look for recurring themes or issues.
- **Be prepared to pivot**: If the data suggests that your product or service is not resonating with customers, be ready to pivot. Don't fall in love with an idea that isn't working. Instead, make the necessary changes to meet the needs of your audience.

Pivoting or Evolving Your Business Based on Real Data, Not Assumptions

One of the biggest mistakes you can make as an entrepreneur is to cling to a flawed idea because you're too attached to it. This is where **pivoting** becomes important. **Pivoting** doesn't mean giving up—it means evolving based on the real-world data you've gathered from customers.

1. When to Pivot: Signs Your Idea Isn't Working

If you're seeing a consistent pattern of negative feedback, low engagement, or poor sales despite your best efforts, it might be time to **pivot**. Pivoting means changing a key aspect of your business model, product, or approach to better align with market demand.

- **Sales are flat**: If your product isn't selling after trying multiple marketing strategies, it might not be meeting customer needs.
- **Customer feedback is negative**: If customers are consistently saying that your product doesn't meet their needs or that there's a better solution elsewhere, it's time to take a hard look at what needs to change.
- **Market trends have shifted**: If new trends or technologies are changing the landscape of your industry, consider adapting your business model to stay relevant.

2. The Power of Data-Driven Decisions

Pivoting doesn't mean guessing what might work next—it means using the data you've collected to make informed decisions. By analyzing customer feedback, behavior, and market trends, you can identify the most viable direction for your business.

- **Conduct customer interviews**: Speak directly with your customers to uncover deeper insights that the data alone might not reveal.
- **Evaluate your competitors**: Look at how other businesses in your space are evolving and find ways to differentiate yourself.

3. Evolving Gradually, Not Drastically

You don't need to completely reinvent your business every time something isn't working. Often, **small tweaks** can have a big impact. By evolving gradually, you can adapt to market changes without losing the essence of your original idea.

- **Refine your product, not abandon it**: If your customers are pointing out specific pain points, address those, rather than scrapping your entire concept.
- **Test changes incrementally**: Roll out small changes and monitor how they affect your business. This allows you to make informed adjustments without disrupting your operations.

Key Message

Ignoring customer feedback is one of the fastest ways to derail your business. By continuously seeking input, testing your ideas early on, and being ready to pivot when necessary, you set yourself up for long-term success. **The key is to listen— because your customers will tell you exactly what they want.** The question is, are you ready to hear it?

The Perils of Growth – Scaling Too Quickly

Every entrepreneur dreams of growth. The idea of seeing your business grow from a small startup to an industry leader is thrilling. It's tempting to think that the sooner you scale, the sooner you'll hit the big time. But here's the brutal truth: **rushing to scale too quickly can be a fatal mistake for startups.**

Scaling without the proper foundation can lead to disaster— overextending your resources, over-promising to customers, and burning out your team. The key to long-term success isn't just about growing fast; it's about scaling **responsibly** and **sustainably**.

In this section, we'll take a deep dive into why scaling too quickly can cause chaos for your startup, how to recognize when it's time to scale, and how to do so without jeopardizing the future of your business.

Why Rushing to Scale is Often a Fatal Mistake for Startups

The desire to expand is natural, but it's often driven by the allure of **quick success** and **external validation**. Scaling too early is like building a house on a shaky foundation—you might get a couple of good floors, but eventually, the whole structure will collapse. Here's why you should think twice before trying to scale your startup too quickly:

1. Lack of a Proven Product-Market Fit

Before you scale, you need to ensure that your product or service is **resonating** with your target market. If you don't have product-market fit, scaling is like putting a Band-Aid on a leaking dam—it won't solve the problem, and it'll only make things worse.

- **Not enough customer validation**: Scaling without understanding whether customers truly value your product or service is risky. If you can't generate consistent demand from a smaller audience, how will you handle a larger one?
- **Market confusion**: Rushing into new markets or expanding your offerings too soon can confuse customers who aren't clear on what your business stands for or what it does. This can lead to missed opportunities and weak brand positioning.

2. Financial Strain and Resource Drain

Scaling requires resources—money, talent, systems, and infrastructure. If you don't have a strong financial foundation, scaling too quickly can strain your budget, deplete your cash reserves, and leave you with insufficient runway to survive.

- **Increased overhead**: Expanding too fast requires hiring more people, investing in marketing campaigns, or increasing inventory. If you don't have the revenue to support these investments, you're taking on too much financial risk.
- **Diluted focus**: Growing too fast can result in taking on more work than your team can handle, leading to poor execution, missed deadlines, and a breakdown in quality control.

3. Customer Experience Takes a Hit

When you scale, you need to ensure that your **customer experience** doesn't suffer. A big part of your initial success is likely due to personal connections with customers and a hands-on approach to solving their problems. Scaling without the right systems in place can result in a drop in service quality, frustrating your customers and damaging your reputation.

- **Decreased service levels**: A sudden surge in customers can overwhelm your team, leading to delayed responses, mistakes, and subpar experiences.
- **Loss of personal touch**: As your business grows, it can be easy to lose sight of the intimate connection you had with

your early customers. This can lead to feelings of neglect among loyal supporters.

The Dangers of Overextending Your Resources

When scaling too quickly, startups often attempt to do everything at once. This can lead to overextending your resources—whether it's your time, cash flow, or talent. Here's why it's important to scale at a pace that matches your **capacity**:

1. Cash Flow Crisis

Scaling requires a significant investment of money. Whether it's hiring more staff, developing new products, or ramping up marketing efforts, growth demands cash—and if you're not careful, it can drain your financial reserves.

- **Running out of capital**: Expanding too fast before achieving steady cash flow can lead to running out of money. Without proper financial planning, you could find yourself struggling to cover operating costs.
- **Unpredictable revenue**: If your revenue doesn't increase in proportion to your scaling efforts, you could end up with significant debt. Managing cash flow becomes a balancing act that can make or break your business.

2. Burnout and Team Overload

As a startup grows, so do the demands on your team. If you don't have the right resources, it's easy for your team to feel overwhelmed, especially if you're scaling at an unsustainable rate. This can lead to burnout and high employee turnover.

- **Staff fatigue**: Scaling quickly means more work, and if your team is stretched too thin, their productivity will drop. What started as enthusiasm and excitement can turn into exhaustion and frustration.
- **Overworked leadership**: As the founder or business owner, you might think you can do everything yourself, but scaling demands a lot of time and energy. Overloading yourself with tasks can result in poor decision-making, lost opportunities, and a breakdown in communication.

3. Loss of Control

As your business expands, you might find it harder to maintain control over every aspect of operations. Without systems and processes in place, this can lead to **disorganization** and **chaos**.

- **Operational inefficiencies**: Scaling without efficient systems and processes can create confusion and waste. This is particularly true if your business relies on manual processes that aren't scalable.
- **Compromised quality**: Without proper checks and balances, the quality of your product or service can slip as you focus on growth rather than maintaining standards.

How to Scale Responsibly and Sustainably

Scaling your business is not a sprint—it's a marathon. To ensure long-term success, it's critical to scale **responsibly** and **sustainably**. Here are some key strategies for scaling at the right pace:

1. Achieve Product-Market Fit First

Before you even think about scaling, you need to ensure that you've found a **solid product-market fit**. This means confirming that your product resonates with your target market, and that there's consistent demand for it.

- **Customer validation**: Test and retest your offering with real customers before scaling. This will help ensure that your product has the potential to meet the needs of a larger market.
- **Refining your offer**: Iterate on your product based on feedback from your initial customers. This might involve tweaking the design, adjusting the pricing, or improving features before going big.

2. Build Scalable Systems

Scaling is all about having the **right systems and processes** in place. This ensures that you can handle growth without sacrificing quality or efficiency. If you're growing faster than you can streamline operations, you risk creating a bottleneck.

- **Automate and delegate**: Invest in tools and software that can automate repetitive tasks. This will free up your time and allow your team to focus on higher-level work.
- **Standardize workflows**: As you expand, having standardized workflows will help ensure consistency and quality control.

3. Focus on Sustainable Growth Metrics

Instead of focusing on growth for growth's sake, keep an eye on **sustainable growth metrics**. This means considering the long-term health of your business, rather than just short-term gains.

- **Cash flow over revenue**: Make sure your business can generate consistent cash flow to fund expansion. Revenue is important, but it doesn't matter if you can't turn it into profit.
- **Customer retention**: Scaling isn't just about acquiring new customers—it's about keeping the ones you have. Focus on customer retention strategies to build a loyal base that can fuel sustainable growth.

Key Message

The rush to scale is seductive, but without the right foundation, it's a trap. Growing too quickly can drain your resources, damage your reputation, and destroy your business in ways you didn't anticipate. **Scaling responsibly means taking it one step at a time, building systems, validating your assumptions, and focusing on sustainable growth**. By

following these principles, you'll be able to grow your business
at a pace that ensures long-term success.

Chapter 5: The Road to Longevity – Ensuring Long-Term Success and Avoiding Collapse

The Importance of Adaptability

I n the world of startups, one thing is certain: **change is inevitable.** The market, technology, customer preferences, and even your competition will evolve in ways you can't predict. If you're not willing to adapt, your business could easily become irrelevant before it ever reaches its full potential.

Adaptability isn't just a nice-to-have trait for business owners—it's an essential skill. The ability to pivot, shift direction when needed, and respond to unforeseen challenges will determine whether your business survives the ups and downs of the startup journey.

In this section, we'll explore why adaptability is crucial, how to stay relevant in a constantly shifting market, and why creating a culture of continuous learning is key to future-proofing your business.

Why You Must Be Willing to Pivot or Change Direction

Business plans are important. **Vision** and **mission** are vital. But no matter how much you plan or how strong your initial idea is, things will **not** go according to plan. And that's okay. In fact, it's often a sign of success if you're able to **pivot** and adapt in the face of new information or changing circumstances.

1. Market Conditions Are Always Shifting

Customer preferences, market trends, and economic land-scapes don't stay static. Just think about the massive shifts we've seen in industries like tech, media, and retail in the past decade alone.

- **Consumer demands change**: What customers wanted five years ago may not be relevant today. To stay ahead, you need to constantly be listening to your customers and adapting to their needs.
- **Tech disruptions**: New technologies can disrupt entire industries. If you're not keeping an eye on emerging technologies or innovations, your business could quickly be outpaced by competitors who are more adaptable.
- **Economic and cultural shifts**: The market doesn't just change based on business cycles—it changes based on larger cultural, social, and political events. The pandemic is a perfect example of how rapidly things can shift, and businesses that were able to adapt flourished while others struggled to survive.

2. It's Not Failure—It's Learning

When you pivot, it's not a sign of failure—it's a sign that you're **learning** and **responding** to the market. The businesses that succeed long-term aren't necessarily those that never stumble— they're the ones that are willing to **learn from mistakes**, **correct their course**, and **pivot** when necessary.

- **Data-driven decisions**: Pivoting is often about understanding what isn't working and using data to guide your new direction. It's about turning failures into stepping stones for success.
- **Test-and-learn mentality**: Businesses that remain rigid in their plans are often the ones that fail. Those that embrace experimentation, measure results, and adjust accordingly are the ones that adapt and thrive.

How to Stay Relevant in a Constantly Changing Market

Staying relevant means understanding that the world around you is in flux, and the business landscape is no exception. How can you ensure your business continues to thrive, even when everything else is changing?

1. Continuously Monitor the Market and Industry Trends

The best way to stay relevant is to stay informed. That means keeping an ear to the ground and being aware of shifts in your industry, as well as in the broader economy.

- **Market research**: Invest in regular market research—this doesn't just mean conducting surveys or reading reports; it means actively engaging with customers, observing your competitors, and following the latest trends.
- **Industry news**: Follow blogs, podcasts, and social media accounts that are at the forefront of industry trends. If you're not staying updated, you risk being blindsided by changes you could've anticipated.
- **Customer behavior**: Keep track of how customer needs and desires are changing. If you can predict those shifts early, you can adjust your product or service before it becomes a need, rather than a response to a trend.

2. Be Willing to Experiment and Innovate

Staying relevant requires you to be open to **experimentation**. Not every idea will work, but if you aren't experimenting, you won't know what might.

- **Small-scale testing**: Run pilots or beta tests with new ideas or products. By testing on a small scale, you can gauge how well it resonates with your audience and make adjustments before fully launching.
- **Adapt the model**: Don't be afraid to modify your product

or service offering. If customer feedback shows a gap in your service, don't delay—take action to fill that gap, even if it means altering your business model or changing your marketing approach.

- **Iterate frequently**: Innovation is not a one-time thing; it's an ongoing process. Constantly seek opportunities to improve your offering and make incremental adjustments to keep pace with market needs.

3. Build Flexibility into Your Business Model

A rigid business model can quickly become outdated, especially in a world where industries are in flux and technology evolves at lightning speed. Building **flexibility** into your business model helps you remain adaptable, no matter the challenges ahead.

- **Modular strategies**: Rather than putting all your eggs in one basket, build modular, flexible strategies that can be easily adapted or changed without causing major disruption.
- **Diversify your revenue streams**: Having multiple sources of revenue gives you the flexibility to shift focus if one stream is underperforming. For example, if you're primarily reliant on one product or service, branching out into complementary offerings can buffer against market shifts.
- **Leverage technology**: Invest in scalable technologies that allow for adjustments as the market changes. Whether it's CRM tools, automation software, or analytics platforms, these tools can help your business stay nimble and respon-

sive.

Developing a Culture of Continuous Learning and Improvement

Businesses that thrive in the long term aren't just adaptable—they're also committed to **continuous learning**. Whether it's learning from your customers, your failures, or your competition, a growth mindset will ensure that you're constantly evolving and improving.

1. Foster a Growth Mindset

As the business leader, you set the tone for your company's culture. Encourage a mindset where everyone—from the CEO to the newest intern—views challenges as **learning opportunities**, not insurmountable obstacles.

- **Accept feedback**: Encourage open feedback loops and constructive criticism. The more feedback you get from your team and customers, the better you can improve and adjust.
- **Celebrate failures**: Emphasize that failure is a part of the learning process. In fact, failures often provide the best lessons, which can lead to greater innovation and problem-solving down the road.
- **Create a safe environment**: Employees need to feel comfortable experimenting and making mistakes. Without this psychological safety, people will be hesitant to contribute new ideas or take risks.

2. Invest in Training and Development

Continuous learning isn't just about theory—it's about action. Invest in regular training and development opportunities for yourself and your team.

- **Skill development**: In an ever-changing business landscape, it's critical that your team has the skills needed to stay competitive. Invest in training programs to improve technical and soft skills.
- **Industry seminars and events**: Attend industry events, conferences, and networking opportunities. These experiences provide fresh insights into trends, innovations, and shifts happening in your field.
- **Encourage self-learning**: Empower employees to continue learning independently. This could mean supporting them in taking online courses, reading books, or pursuing certifications relevant to your business.

3. Lead by Example

As the founder or CEO, you are the face of the culture you want to create. If you embrace learning, adaptability, and flexibility, your team will follow suit.

- **Demonstrate resilience**: Show your team how to respond to setbacks and challenges with a positive attitude. Your ability to adapt to changing circumstances will set the standard for how your team handles adversity.
- **Stay curious**: Never stop learning yourself. Whether it's through reading, mentoring, or seeking advice from others,

the more you learn, the more you can inspire your team to do the same.

- **Encourage experimentation**: Take risks and try new things in your business. When your team sees you stepping out of your comfort zone, they'll feel empowered to do the same.

Key Message

In a world where everything is constantly changing, **adaptability** is no longer optional—it's a critical survival skill. Whether it's pivoting your business model, staying on top of market trends, or fostering a culture of continuous learning, adaptability is key to ensuring your startup can thrive no matter what challenges come your way. By staying flexible, open to feedback, and willing to evolve, you'll position your business for long-term success in a fast-changing world.

Building a Team That Works

As a business owner, one of the most important and often overlooked aspects of your success is **building the right team**. The reality is, no matter how great your idea is or how driven you are, you can't do it alone. At some point, you'll need to bring in people who share your vision, help carry the load, and contribute their unique expertise to make your business thrive.

But building a team isn't just about hiring a few people and crossing your fingers. It's about **creating the right environment**, **managing people effectively**, and ensuring that everyone is aligned with the company's goals, even when the road gets tough.

In this section, we'll dive into the often-overlooked realities of hiring and managing a team, discuss how to avoid the trap of being the "lone wolf" entrepreneur, and explore the critical importance of maintaining a **strong company culture**.

The Reality of Hiring and Managing People as a Business Owner

Hiring the right people is both a **science** and an **art**. As a startup founder, you're not just looking for employees; you're looking for partners who will help bring your vision to life and carry the weight of your dreams. The **reality** is that building a strong team requires constant effort, good judgment, and a deep understanding of what your business needs—both today and in the future.

1. Finding the Right Fit

As your business grows, you'll need to hire people who not only have the technical skills but also align with your company's **values**, **culture**, and **mission**. The wrong hire can drain your energy, waste resources, and disrupt the balance you're trying to create.

- **Skills vs. culture fit**: The ideal team members are those who not only bring the necessary skills to the table but also share the values and work ethic that define your company. It's important to find people who are adaptable, positive, and able to grow with the business.
- **Hiring for growth**: As your company expands, your team needs to be able to scale with it. Always look for people who

can grow into new roles, take on additional responsibilities, and help build a sustainable foundation.

- **Interviewing smartly**: Don't just rely on resumes. Take the time to **interview deeply**, ask about past experiences, and test for cultural fit through realistic scenarios. Also, don't be afraid to **trust your instincts**—if someone doesn't feel right, it's okay to pass.

2. Delegating Effectively

One of the biggest challenges new entrepreneurs face is the temptation to **do everything themselves**. Early on, you might be the marketer, salesperson, accountant, and CEO all in one. But this is **unsustainable** and counterproductive.

- **Let go of control**: The sooner you realize that you can't do everything yourself, the better. Learn to delegate effectively and trust your team members to handle tasks they're good at. Letting go of the small stuff will free you up to focus on **strategic growth**.
- **Empower your team**: Giving your team ownership over certain projects or areas of your business not only helps with delegation but also **builds trust** and makes them feel valued. When people are trusted, they perform better.
- **Know when to ask for help**: Hiring and managing people is not a solo job. Seek out mentors, advisors, or HR experts who can help guide you through the nuances of building a strong team.

How to Avoid the Trap of Trying to Do Everything Yourself

Entrepreneurs often fall into the **hero syndrome**, thinking that if they don't personally handle everything, their business will fail. But trying to juggle every task is not only draining—it's also counterproductive. **The truth is, you can't scale your business alone**.

1. Recognize Your Limitations

It's easy to fall into the trap of believing that no one can do things as well as you can. But trying to do everything yourself is a recipe for burnout.

- **Outsource when needed**: You can't be an expert in everything, and that's okay. Outsource tasks that don't require your direct involvement—whether it's accounting, social media management, or graphic design—so you can focus on what's important.
- **Leverage your team's strengths**: Every team member brings something unique to the table. Trust them to do the work you hired them for. Often, others will bring fresh perspectives and ideas that can **improve your business**.
- **Accept help**: Don't be afraid to ask for help from advisors or mentors. You don't need to do it all alone—there are people who've walked this path before and can offer guidance and wisdom.

2. Focus on Your Core Competencies

As the founder, your time is best spent on activities that directly contribute to the **growth** and **vision** of your company. Don't waste time micromanaging or getting bogged down in operational tasks that someone else can handle.

- **Set priorities**: Identify what only **you** can do—whether it's business development, product innovation, or strategy—and focus your efforts there. Everything else can be delegated or outsourced.
- **Limit your distractions**: Eliminate tasks that don't directly contribute to the long-term success of the business. Saying "no" is hard, but it's essential for maintaining your focus.
- **Delegate non-core tasks**: From customer service to day-to-day administration, make sure that non-strategic tasks are handled by the appropriate person, freeing you up for high-level thinking and growth.

Creating a Strong Company Culture and Maintaining Morale During Tough Times

A business isn't just about the product or service—it's about the people who make it happen. A strong company culture and high morale are **foundational elements** that can either make or break your startup.

1. Define Your Core Values

One of the first things you need to do is define what your company stands for. What values will guide every decision, interaction, and behavior? A strong company culture is built on clear, shared values.

- **Create a mission statement**: A clear, inspiring mission statement gives your team a sense of purpose and direction. It's the "why" behind what you're doing.
- **Communicate the vision**: Make sure everyone on the team understands the bigger picture and how their work contributes to it. When people feel connected to the mission, they're more engaged.
- **Lead by example**: As the business owner, you set the tone for the company culture. Be the example of the behaviors you want to see—whether it's transparency, accountability, or innovation.

2. Foster a Positive Work Environment

A positive work environment is essential to keeping morale high and ensuring that your team feels motivated, even when things get tough.

- **Celebrate small wins**: Don't just focus on the big milestones. Celebrate the small wins and everyday successes to keep your team feeling recognized and appreciated.
- **Provide opportunities for growth**: Offer training, professional development, and opportunities for advancement. People want to feel like they're growing, not just working.

- **Encourage collaboration**: A sense of camaraderie is crucial in a startup. Foster an environment where team members feel comfortable sharing ideas, offering feedback, and collaborating.

3. Managing Morale During Tough Times

The startup journey is full of ups and downs. During tough times, it's important to keep your team motivated and remind them why they're part of the company.

- **Be transparent**: Communicate openly with your team about the challenges you're facing. Transparency fosters trust and keeps people from feeling left in the dark.
- **Show appreciation**: During tough times, show extra appreciation for your team's efforts. Recognize the hard work they're putting in, even when results aren't immediate.
- **Encourage balance**: Encourage your team to take care of themselves. Overworking leads to burnout, and the more you encourage balance, the more productive and motivated your team will be in the long run.

Key Message

Building a successful business isn't just about having a great idea—it's about having the right people alongside you, working together to bring that idea to life. Hiring, managing, and fostering a positive company culture are just as important as your product or service. Remember, **you can't do it all on your own**, and building a team that shares your vision, works together, and thrives in both good times and bad is crucial for long-term success. So, hire wisely, delegate effectively, and never underestimate the power of a strong, motivated team.

Planning for the Unexpected

Starting and running a business is a thrilling rollercoaster ride, full of highs and lows. But as every seasoned entrepreneur will tell you, the unexpected is always lurking just around the corner. Whether it's an economic downturn, a global crisis, or a sudden change in market conditions, the **unpredictable** is one of the few things you can count on in business. While you can't predict the future, you **can** prepare for it.

In this section, we'll discuss how to protect your business from unforeseen challenges, the importance of having contingency plans in place, and why diversifying your revenue streams is more than just a good idea—it's a lifeline when hard times hit.

How to Protect Your Business from Economic Downturns or Unexpected Events

Economic downturns, recessions, and global disruptions (like a pandemic) can send shockwaves through industries and businesses, often causing massive setbacks. But some businesses are better equipped to weather these storms than others. How? **Preparation**.

1. Building Financial Resilience

Financial resilience is the ability to endure and rebound from economic challenges. Having a solid **cash reserve** or **emergency fund** can be the difference between weathering a storm or closing your doors.

- **Set aside a financial cushion**: Aim to have enough cash reserves to cover at least **three to six months of operating expenses**. This will give you a safety net if sales drop suddenly or unexpected costs arise.
- **Cut unnecessary expenses**: Review your expenses regularly to identify areas where you can cut back or eliminate waste. Having lean operations gives you more flexibility in times of uncertainty.
- **Diversify investments**: If your business has investments, look at diversifying them. Relying on a single asset or source of income can be risky when the market fluctuates.

2. Evaluating and Strengthening Your Supply Chain

Economic downturns often expose weaknesses in the supply chain, whether it's from global disruptions, supplier shutdowns, or delivery delays. Protecting your supply chain is key to keeping your business operational.

- **Assess supplier vulnerability**: Evaluate how dependent you are on specific suppliers or manufacturers. Diversifying your supplier base can help mitigate risks if one supplier faces difficulties.
- **Negotiate flexible terms**: If possible, negotiate flexible

payment terms with suppliers or partners. This will help you maintain cash flow if you need to delay or adjust payments in tough times.

- **Stock up strategically**: For some businesses, having a bit more inventory on hand can provide a buffer during supply chain disruptions, but don't overstock—just enough to prevent immediate issues.

The Importance of Having Contingency Plans and Insurance

The phrase "hope for the best, plan for the worst" should be your guiding principle when it comes to unexpected events. **Contingency plans** are essential for ensuring that your business can continue operating if the worst happens.

1. Creating Contingency Plans for Major Risks

A contingency plan outlines the steps to take when things go wrong—whether it's a natural disaster, market crash, or something more personal, like a key employee leaving. If you wait until disaster strikes to start planning, it might be too late.

- **Identify your top risks**: Start by identifying what could go wrong in your business. Are you dependent on seasonal sales? What happens if a competitor releases a disruptive product? What if your supplier has a major setback? Anticipate the worst-case scenarios so you can create specific plans for each.
- **Write down your action plan**: For each risk, develop a detailed action plan. This could include having a sec-

ondary revenue stream to offset losses, backup suppliers, or emergency communication plans.

- **Assign responsibility**: Make sure your team knows exactly who's responsible for executing each part of the contingency plan. Having clear lines of responsibility helps things move quickly when time is critical.

2. Investing in Insurance

Insurance is an often-overlooked aspect of business planning, but it can provide **peace of mind** and **financial protection** in the event of unforeseen circumstances. Without the proper insurance, your business may be at risk of going under if disaster strikes.

- **Types of business insurance**: Depending on your industry, consider general liability insurance, property insurance, professional liability, and business interruption insurance. Research the types that will cover the unique risks your business faces.
- **Review coverage regularly**: Don't assume your initial insurance plan is enough. Regularly review your coverage to ensure it matches the scale and scope of your business, especially as your business grows.
- **Insurance is not a "set it and forget it"**: Make sure you fully understand what your policies cover and the fine print. Working with an insurance advisor can ensure you're not leaving yourself vulnerable to a gap in coverage.

Why Diversifying Revenue Streams Can Save Your Business in Hard Times

Relying on a single revenue stream is like building your house on sand. It might look fine at first, but when the tide comes in, it's more likely to wash away. Diversifying your revenue streams ensures that you have backup income in place if one stream dries up, and it can help smooth over the fluctuations in the market.

1. Expanding Product and Service Offerings

One of the best ways to diversify is by expanding your **product or service portfolio**. You might start with one core offering, but what happens if market demand shifts? Having multiple revenue-generating products or services means you'll be able to weather fluctuations more easily.

- **Evaluate your market**: Look for gaps in your existing market. What additional products or services can you offer your current customers that would align with your brand?
- **Test new ideas**: Before committing fully to new products, test them in small ways—whether through a pilot program or limited release. This allows you to gather feedback without risking too much capital.
- **Create recurring income models**: Subscription models or membership programs are an effective way to stabilize cash flow, especially during periods of market uncertainty.

2. Exploring New Markets

If your business is heavily reliant on one market, you may want to consider diversifying into **new geographical regions** or **different customer segments**. Expanding your reach can help cushion the blow when one segment faces downturns.

- **Research new demographics**: Your current market may be limited by geography, income, or other factors. Are there untapped customer bases that would benefit from your product or service?
- **Test new markets cautiously**: Expanding into new markets can be risky, but it can be done safely by conducting **market research** and **pilot testing** before going all-in.
- **Leverage online channels**: If you're geographically limited, explore expanding your reach online. E-commerce, social media marketing, and remote services can help you tap into a global market without major upfront costs.

3. Creating Strategic Partnerships

Strategic partnerships can also diversify your revenue streams by bringing in additional income sources without having to create new products or services yourself. Joint ventures and partnerships with other businesses can be mutually beneficial.

- **Collaborate with complementary businesses**: Find businesses that offer products or services that complement yours. This opens up new cross-selling opportunities and increases your exposure to new customers.
- **Create affiliate programs**: If your product or service

lends itself to affiliate marketing, consider launching an affiliate program where others can promote your product in exchange for a commission.

- **Leverage brand partnerships**: Partnering with well-established brands can bring instant credibility to your business and open doors to new revenue opportunities.

Key Message

No one can predict the future, but with the right strategies in place, you can be prepared for whatever comes your way. **Planning for the unexpected** isn't about being paranoid; it's about **ensuring business continuity**, protecting your financial health, and minimizing risk. By building financial resilience, having contingency plans, investing in insurance, and diversifying revenue streams, you'll increase your chances of weathering the inevitable storms that will come your way. The unexpected is going to happen—prepare for it, and you'll be ready to handle whatever comes your way.

Chapter 6: These Are the Hard Truths – 20 Small Business Facts You Need to Know

You wanted them, here they are...

1. Starting a Business is Risky

- More than 20% of new businesses fail within the first year.
- You are taking on financial risk, personal stress, and uncertainty when starting a business.

2. Cash Flow is the Lifeblood of Your Business

- Many businesses fail due to poor cash flow management, not a lack of profit.
- You must ensure that your income always exceeds your expenses, or your business will quickly collapse.

3. The First 3-5 Years Are the Hardest

- The initial years of running a business are often filled with trial and error, mistakes, and low profits.
- You will likely face major financial struggles during the startup phase.

4. Entrepreneurs Work More Hours Than Anyone Else

- Expect to work long hours—much more than a typical 9-to-5 job.
- Work-life balance will be hard to maintain, especially in the early stages.

5. You Will Face Unexpected Costs

- Startups often underestimate the cost of equipment, marketing, insurance, and employee benefits.
- There will always be unexpected expenses that will test your financial planning.

6. You Won't Have a Paycheck at First

- Many new business owners don't take a salary for months (or even years) while their company stabilizes.
- Be prepared for financial strain and personal sacrifices.

7. Marketing Is a Constant Job

- Marketing is never "done." You will need a continuous strategy for customer acquisition, brand awareness, and engagement.
- Without strong marketing, your business will struggle to grow.

8. Not Everyone Will Support You

- Friends and family may not always understand or support your decision to start a business.
- Be prepared for skepticism, criticism, or even discouragement from those around you.

9. Your Business Will Demand More Than Just a "Great Idea"

- Even the best idea won't succeed without solid execution, strong management, and resilience.
- Starting a business requires much more than just passion or creativity.

10. You'll Need to Wear Many Hats

- As a small business owner, you'll be responsible for everything from sales to accounting to customer service.
- Don't expect to delegate everything at first; you'll have to do most tasks yourself.

11. The Competition Will Be Fierce

- No matter what industry you enter, expect competition.
- Even if your product or service is unique, there will always be someone trying to take your customers.

12. Failure Is Common – Learn from It

- Most entrepreneurs will fail at some point. The key is to learn from your mistakes and keep moving forward.
- Failure is not the end, but an essential part of the entrepreneurial process.

13. You May Struggle to Find Employees

- It's difficult to find talented employees willing to work for a small, unknown company.
- You'll often need to hire individuals who are passionate but may not have all the skills you want.

14. You'll Have to Compete with Big Players

- Even as a small business, you may have to go head-to-head with large corporations that have more resources.
- You must find ways to differentiate yourself and provide unique value to customers.

15. Legal Issues Are Inevitable

- Whether it's setting up your business legally, signing contracts, or dealing with intellectual property, legal challenges are part of the game.
- You'll likely need a lawyer or legal advisor to navigate the complexities.

16. You'll Need Capital – A Lot of It

- Most businesses require capital for startup costs, ongoing expenses, and growth.
- You'll need to explore funding options, including personal savings, loans, or investors.

17. Customer Retention is Harder Than Acquisition

- While it's important to attract customers, keeping them is even more challenging.
- You must offer exceptional customer service and continually innovate to maintain customer loyalty.

18. Many Businesses Fail Due to Poor Management

- Strong leadership and decision-making skills are essential to the success of your business.
- Effective management, planning, and problem-solving can make or break your company.

19. You Will Be Responsible for Everything – Including Your Mental Health

- Entrepreneurs face mental and emotional pressure that can lead to burnout, anxiety, or depression.
- Taking care of your mental health and setting boundaries is just as important as running your business.

20. Success Takes Time – Don't Expect Instant Gratification

- Building a profitable and sustainable business takes time.
- Instant success is rare, and most businesses need years of dedication before reaching their full potential.

Key Message

These 20 hard truths are essential for any entrepreneur to understand before starting a business. Knowing these facts can help you navigate the challenges that come with entrepreneurship and set realistic expectations for the journey ahead. By preparing for these realities, you'll be better equipped to face the obstacles and build a thriving business. I would recommend you work toward a strong supportive network both professionally and personally and always, always ensure you have time to balance business with family.

Chapter 7: Embracing the Journey

Your Next Steps as a Startup Founder

The road ahead is rarely smooth. In fact, the entrepreneurial journey can feel more like navigating a **rocky cliffside**—one step forward, two steps sideways, and sometimes a slip or two. But here's the thing: those who **keep going** are the ones who make it. As a startup founder, the key to success is not just about ideas, innovation, or even market timing; it's about **resilience**—your ability to weather the storms and stay in the game long enough to reach your goals.

In this section, we'll dive into how to stay resilient, take immediate action, foster a **growth mindset**, and embrace both the **highs and lows** as part of your entrepreneurial journey. It's about keeping your eyes on the prize, no matter how many setbacks you face. So, let's get started with your next steps.

How to Stay Resilient and Keep Moving Forward, Even When the Going Gets Tough

Building a business is an emotional rollercoaster. One day, you're celebrating a small win, and the next, you're staring down a major setback. How do you stay resilient when it feels like everything is working against you?

1. Develop Mental Toughness

Resilience doesn't just come from pushing through physical exhaustion or stress—it's about **mental toughness**. It's the ability to take a punch, get back up, and keep swinging.

- **Refuse to quit**: No matter how tough things get, remind yourself that **quitting is not an option**. Focus on small daily actions that move you forward. Progress is progress, no matter how small.
- **Frame setbacks as lessons**: The inevitable setbacks aren't failures—they're **lessons**. When things don't go as planned, don't beat yourself up. Instead, ask, "What can I learn from this? How can I improve next time?"
- **Maintain a positive outlook**: Keeping a **positive mindset** doesn't mean ignoring reality—it means choosing to see challenges as opportunities for growth. Surround yourself with positive influences, whether it's people, books, or podcasts.

2. Build a Support Network

Building a support network is critical for maintaining resilience. You can't do this alone.

- **Find mentors**: Seek out those who have been through the entrepreneurial grind. Their wisdom and advice can help you avoid mistakes and maintain perspective when things get tough.
- **Lean on your team**: Your team isn't just there to help execute tasks; they are your emotional and professional **partners in the trenches**. Be honest about challenges, share wins, and lean on each other for support.
- **Join a community**: Online forums, local entrepreneurial groups, and mastermind circles can be great for building a **community of like-minded individuals** who understand the journey and can offer support, ideas, and encouragement.

Practical Advice on Taking Immediate Action with Your New Knowledge

Now that you've absorbed these hard truths and strategies, it's time to **move from knowledge to action**. The **real magic** happens when you apply what you've learned.

1. Set Clear, Actionable Goals

Action without direction is just busywork. Set clear, actionable goals that break your big vision down into manageable steps.

- **Create SMART goals**: Make sure your goals are **Specific, Measurable, Achievable, Relevant, and Time-bound**. For example, instead of "improve cash flow," try "increase monthly revenue by 10% within the next quarter."
- **Break it down**: Break down your goals into smaller, digestible tasks. This makes the process less overwhelming and helps you see progress along the way.
- **Set priorities**: Focus on the highest-impact tasks first. Ask yourself, "What will make the biggest difference in moving my business forward today?"

2. Take Action Every Day

Consistency is the secret ingredient to success. As a startup founder, you won't always feel motivated to act, but **discipline** is what makes success inevitable.

- **Take small steps daily**: You don't have to make massive moves every day. Just keep taking one step forward, no matter how small. That could be sending an email, tweaking your website, or reaching out to a potential partner.
- **Start with the hardest task**: Tackle your hardest task first thing in the morning, when your mind is fresh. The "Eat That Frog" approach works wonders for productivity and preventing procrastination.
- **Learn and iterate**: Take action, gather feedback, and **adjust accordingly**. Don't wait for everything to be perfect—just start, and you'll improve as you go.

Developing a Growth Mindset for Continuous Improvement

A **growth mindset** is the belief that you can improve and grow through effort and learning. As a founder, you must foster this mindset to thrive. It's not about being perfect; it's about being better tomorrow than you are today.

1. Embrace Learning and Adaptation

The world of business is constantly changing. To stay ahead of the curve, you need to **embrace lifelong learning**.

- **Stay curious**: The most successful entrepreneurs are **constantly learning**. Whether it's reading books, attending workshops, or learning from competitors, always be in "learning mode."
- **Welcome challenges**: A growth mindset thrives in challenges. When you face difficulties, see them as opportunities to improve. Ask yourself, "What is this situation teaching me?"
- **Seek feedback**: Don't shy away from feedback, whether it's from customers, mentors, or team members. Feedback is the **fuel for improvement**.

2. Stay Humble and Open to Change

When you're building a business, it's easy to become too attached to your original vision or idea. But businesses often evolve over time, and flexibility is key to success.

- **Adapt to change**: The ability to pivot and change your strategy when necessary is crucial. Markets, technologies, and customer preferences evolve, and so should your business.
- **Let go of the ego**: Don't be afraid to admit when something isn't working. It's not a reflection of you—it's part of the process. **Letting go of your ego** allows you to adapt more quickly.
- **Celebrate progress, not perfection**: Instead of constantly seeking perfection, celebrate the progress you make along the way. Acknowledge how far you've come, even if you haven't reached the destination yet.

How to Embrace Both the Highs and Lows of Entrepreneurship as Part of Your Journey

Entrepreneurship is a **rollercoaster ride**—and that's what makes it exciting. It's not all sunshine and rainbows, but it's also not all doom and gloom. Embrace the full experience—the **highs and lows**, the wins and losses—because each moment is part of the journey.

1. Celebrate Your Wins

It's easy to get caught up in the grind and forget to celebrate your successes, no matter how small. **Take time to acknowledge your wins** and reflect on how far you've come.

- **Mark milestones**: Whether it's your first paying customer, your first partnership, or reaching your revenue goal, celebrate these wins. This will keep you motivated for the next challenge.
- **Share your success**: Celebrate with your team and your support network. Their encouragement can fuel your next big leap.
- **Reflect on the journey**: Take a step back and look at how far you've come. Give yourself credit for the work you've put in and the obstacles you've overcome.

2. Manage the Lows with Grace

The lows will come. And when they do, don't let them crush your spirit. The key is how you **respond**.

- **Ride the waves**: When things go wrong, remind yourself that it's temporary. View the low points as part of the process, not as a reason to quit.
- **Stay focused on the long-term vision**: Keep your eye on the bigger picture. Short-term setbacks are just that—**short-term**. Don't lose sight of the journey you're on.

- **Lean into your support system**: Don't go through the tough times alone. Talk to your mentors, peers, and team members. Sometimes just sharing your struggles can lighten the load.

Key Message

As you move forward in your entrepreneurial journey, remember that building a business isn't about avoiding failure—it's about **embracing it as part of the process**. With the right mindset, the right actions, and the right support, you can make your dreams a reality. So, take the next step—stay resilient, keep learning, and embrace the journey. The highs and lows will shape you into the business leader you need to be.

Your Entrepreneurial Journey Starts Now!

Congratulations! You've just completed **Brutal Truths About Starting a Business**. You've gained the hard-won insights, strategies, and knowledge that can help you navigate the tricky waters of entrepreneurship. But more importantly, you've taken the first step toward turning your business dreams into reality.

Starting a business is no easy feat, and throughout this book, we've explored the realities that most aspiring entrepreneurs don't want to face. We've talked about:

- **The mental shift from employee to entrepreneur**: Understanding that being a business owner means adapting to a new mindset and learning to embrace uncertainty, risk, and the emotional rollercoaster that comes with it.
- **The importance of a solid plan**: Why having a business plan is non-negotiable, and how to create one that keeps you focused and accountable in a constantly changing environment.
- **The hard truths of startup life**: The financial strain, burnout, time commitment, and personal sacrifices that come with building a business—and how to manage them

to ensure long-term success.

- **Practical steps and actionable advice**: How to take immediate action, overcome fear, manage cash flow, deal with setbacks, and adapt to the unexpected.
- **Key pitfalls to avoid**: The dangers of scaling too quickly, ignoring customer feedback, and underestimating the time and effort it takes to get your business off the ground.

Now, armed with this knowledge, you're better prepared to tackle the challenges ahead and avoid the mistakes that often derail startup dreams. You know that success doesn't come overnight, and that building a business is a marathon, not a sprint. But with persistence, resilience, and a willingness to keep learning and adapting, you can achieve your goals.

Thank You for Your Time

I want to take a moment to **thank you** for investing your time in reading this book and taking the first step toward your entrepreneurial journey. I know you have a lot of options when it comes to business books, and I appreciate that you chose to dive into **Brutal Truths About Starting a Business**.

As you move forward with your business, remember that every successful entrepreneur has had to face the same tough lessons. The difference between those who succeed and those who don't isn't talent or luck—it's the **willingness to push through** when it feels impossible, and the determination to keep improving, learning, and adapting.

So, get out there and start taking action. Use what you've learned, make mistakes, learn from them, and keep moving forward. Your business journey is just beginning, and I believe you have what it takes to make it.

Share Your Experience: Leave a Review

If you found this book helpful, I'd be incredibly grateful if you could take a moment to leave a review on **Amazon**. Your feedback helps other entrepreneurs find this book and equips them with the same tools and insights to succeed in their businesses.

A review can be as simple as a few sentences about what resonated with you or how this book helped you take the next step in your journey. If you think others will benefit from it, please share your thoughts—your words could make all the difference for someone who's just starting out.

Thank you again for choosing this book. I wish you nothing but success as you continue to build, grow, and thrive as an entrepreneur.

Good luck, and keep pushing forward!

P.S. If you're ever feeling stuck or need further guidance on your business journey, don't hesitate to reach out. Keep learning, keep growing, and remember—I believe in you, you've got this!

YOUR ENTREPRENEURIAL JOURNEY STARTS NOW!

Bonus Section: 20-Step Checklist for Starting a Business

H ere's a checklist to guide you through the process:

1. Identify Your Business Idea

- Brainstorm potential business ideas based on your skills, interests, and market gaps.
- Choose an idea that excites you and solves a problem.

2. Conduct Market Research

- Validate your business idea by understanding market demand, customer needs, and competition.
- Research industry trends and identify your target audience.

3. Define Your Business Mission and Vision

- Clearly articulate what your business aims to achieve and the values that will guide it.
- Set long-term goals and define your business's purpose.

4. Develop a Business Plan

- Write a detailed business plan that outlines your vision, mission, products/services, market research, competitive analysis, and financial projections.
- Create short-term and long-term goals to measure your business's progress.

5. Choose a Business Structure

- Decide on a legal structure (e.g., sole proprietorship, partnership, LLC, corporation) based on liability, taxes, and funding needs.
- Consult with a legal professional if necessary.

6. Register Your Business Name

- Choose a unique, memorable name that reflects your brand.
- Check for domain availability and trademarks to ensure the name is legally protected.

7. Register Your Business

- Register your business with the appropriate local, state, or national authorities.
- Obtain an employer identification number (EIN) for tax purposes (if required).

8. Obtain Necessary Licenses and Permits

- Research local, state, and federal regulations and obtain the necessary licenses and permits to operate legally.
- Check industry-specific regulations for compliance.

9. Set Up Your Business Finances

- Open a separate business bank account to keep personal and business finances distinct.
- Set up accounting and bookkeeping systems (or hire a professional accountant).

10. Create a Budget and Financial Plan

- Establish a detailed budget for your startup, including projected expenses and revenue.
- Plan for initial funding and ongoing cash flow needs.

11. Secure Funding

- Explore different funding options such as self-funding, loans, investors, or crowdfunding.
- Prepare a pitch or funding proposal if seeking investors or loans.

12. Set Up Your Business Location

- Decide whether you'll operate from a home office, a rented space, or a storefront.
- Ensure your location complies with zoning laws and is accessible to your target market.

13. Build Your Brand Identity

- Develop a brand strategy that includes your logo, colors, fonts, and tone of voice.
- Create marketing materials (business cards, brochures, etc.) that reflect your brand.

14. Build a Website and Online Presence

- Create a professional website to showcase your products, services, and brand story.
- Set up social media accounts on platforms relevant to your target audience.

15. Set Up Customer Relationship Management (CRM) Systems

- Choose a CRM system to manage customer data, track leads, and improve communication.
- Automate customer follow-up processes to increase sales efficiency.

16. Develop a Marketing Strategy

- Create a marketing plan that includes strategies for online and offline promotion.
- Choose marketing channels (social media, content marketing, paid ads, etc.) that best reach your target audience.

17. Launch Your Product or Service

- Finalize your product or service offerings and prepare for launch.
- Plan a launch event or promotion to create excitement and awareness.

18. Monitor Cash Flow and Expenses

- Regularly track your cash flow to ensure your business remains financially healthy.
- Adjust your budget and expenses as necessary to ensure sustainability.

19. Focus on Customer Service

- Provide exceptional customer service to retain loyal clients and generate positive word-of-mouth.
- Collect customer feedback to improve products, services, and customer experience.

20. Adapt and Scale Your Business

- Continuously evaluate your business performance and be prepared to pivot if necessary.
- Look for opportunities to scale by expanding your product line, reaching new markets, or improving operational efficiency.

Bonus Section 2: Key Competencies During First Six Months

The first six months of a new business are critical for setting the foundation for long-term success. During this period, certain competencies are particularly important for small business entrepreneurs to demonstrate in order to navigate early challenges and create a sustainable business model. Here are the top 5 competencies to focus on during the **first 6 months**:

1. Resilience and Perseverance

- **Why it's important:** The initial phase of entrepreneurship is full of obstacles, from slow customer acquisition to unexpected operational challenges. Resilience allows entrepreneurs to bounce back from setbacks and stay motivated even when things don't go according to plan.
- **How to demonstrate:** Keep pushing forward despite early failures or slow progress. Learn from mistakes, adjust strategies, and remain committed to your business goals.

2. Financial Management

- **Why it's important:** Cash flow problems are one of the leading causes of small business failure, especially in the early stages. In the first six months, entrepreneurs must manage limited resources carefully to ensure survival and lay the groundwork for growth.
- **How to demonstrate:** Create a realistic budget, track every expense, monitor cash flow closely, and manage any funding wisely. Prioritize essential spending and avoid unnecessary expenses to ensure the business remains financially viable.

3. Customer Focus and Market Research

- **Why it's important:** Understanding your target market and ensuring you're solving a real problem is crucial during the early stages. Customer feedback is invaluable in refining products and services to meet market needs and expectations.
- **How to demonstrate:** Engage with early customers, listen to their feedback, and be willing to pivot if necessary. Conduct surveys, interviews, or market tests to understand customer needs and preferences.

4. Time Management and Prioritization

- **Why it's important:** Entrepreneurs wear many hats, especially in the early stages. Managing time effectively allows them to balance product development, marketing, sales, customer service, and administrative tasks without burning out.
- **How to demonstrate:** Create daily and weekly to-do lists, set clear priorities, and focus on high-impact tasks that drive revenue and business growth. Learn to delegate when possible, and avoid getting bogged down in non-essential tasks.

5. Adaptability and Problem-Solving

- **Why it's important:** The first six months are unpredictable, and entrepreneurs must be able to adjust quickly to changing circumstances—whether it's market shifts, unforeseen challenges, or new opportunities.
- **How to demonstrate:** Stay flexible in your approach and be open to changing your business model, marketing strategies, or product offerings based on real-time feedback and new information. Use problems as opportunities to learn and evolve the business.

Key Message

By focusing on these core competencies in the first six months, small business entrepreneurs can establish a strong foundation for future growth, overcome early challenges, and increase their chances of long-term success.

Thanks again and wishing you all of the success in the world. It is there for you so make it happen!

References

- American Express. (2020). *The small business guide to cash flow management.* American Express. https://www.amer icanexpress.com/en-us/business/trends-and-insights/ar ticles/the-small-business-guide-to-cash-flow-manageme nt/
- Blank, S. (2013). *The four steps to the epiphany: Successful strategies for products that win.* K&S Ranch.
- Drucker, P. F. (2006). *Innovation and entrepreneurship: Practice and principles.* HarperBusiness.
- Finkelstein, L. (2018). *Startups: A practical guide to launching a successful startup.* Wiley.
- Harvard Business Review. (2021). *The entrepreneur's guide to success.* Harvard Business Review Press.
- Kiyosaki, R. T. (2011). *Rich dad's guide to starting your own business: How to turn your ideas into cash.* Business Plus.
- McKeown, G. (2014). *Essentialism: The disciplined pursuit of less.* Crown Business.
- Osterwalder, A., & Pigneur, Y. (2010). *Business model generation: A handbook for visionaries, game changers, and challengers.* Wiley.

- Reiss, D. (2020). *The startup playbook: The complete guide to building a business from scratch.* Business Expert Press.
- Young, J. (2021). *The importance of market research for startups.* Forbes. https://www.forbes.com/sites/forbes coachescouncil/2021/02/02/the-importance-of-market-research-for-startups/
- Patel, N., & Solomon, P. (2022). *The lean startup: How to test and scale your business idea in the real world.* Entrepreneur Press.
- Johnson, R. (2023). *Start smart: A comprehensive guide to launching your business in the modern market.* Wiley.